RDSP EDITION

safe and
secure

The strategies offered in this book are provided for the general guidance and benefit of the reader. This book provides information. It does not provide legal advice.

The information contained in the book is accurate at the date of publishing. However, we recommend that readers contact their own professional advisor or consultant when planning to implement any strategies. This will ensure the latest available information is taken into consideration and matched with individual circumstances.

PLAN Institute for Caring Citizenship

PLAN – Planned Lifetime Advocacy Network

260 – 3665 Kingsway

Vancouver, B.C. V5R 5W2

PHONE 604 439-9566   FAX 604 439-7001

www.planinstitute.ca   www.PLAN.ca

This book uses the term "disability" to refer to those challenges, conditions, circumstances, handicaps, and impairments that limit the functional ability of people. As is common in most publications of this kind, the person is the focus, the disability secondary.

Library and Archives Canada Cataloguing in Publication

Etmanski, Al, 1947-

Safe and secure : six steps to creating a good life for people with disabilities / Al Etmanski ; with Vickie Cammack & Jack Collins. — RDSP ed.

ISBN 978-0-9730383-3-0

1. People with disabilities--Family relationships. 2. People with disabilities—Finance, Personal. 3. Estate planning. I. Cammack, Vickie, 1951- II. Collins, Jack, 1929- III. PLAN Institute for Caring Citizenship IV. Title.

HV1568.E85 2009   362.4'043   C2008-907270-7

Editing services by Linda McDaniel

Design and production by www.workingdesign.net

safe and
secure

SIX STEPS TO CREATING
A GOOD LIFE FOR PEOPLE
WITH DISABILITIES

Al Etmanski

with Jack Collins and Vickie Cammack

RDSP contribution by Jack Styan

RDSP EDITION 2008

Acknowledgements

The original contents of this book were inspired by the persistence, passion, and creativity of a remarkable group of individuals and families. My thanks to the founding Board of PLAN: Jack Collins, Dick McCallum, Joan Lawrence, Chuck Walker, Duncan McEwen, Gloria Roberts, Ron Duff, Ernie Bryan, and Anne Saen. A special thanks to our subsequent leaders: Arthur Mudry, Ted Kuntz, and Susan Whittaker.

This RDSP edition is made possible by the Government of British Columbia—in particular, the Ministry of Housing and Social Development— who wants to make sure that every British Columbian with a disability and their family receives a copy of this book. Our government's leadership in harmonizing the new Registered Disability Savings Plan with BC Benefits regulation has set a Canadian standard. Thanks particularly to Cairine MacDonald and Andrew Wharton for respecting and trusting the resilience of individuals and families.

Our thanks to the following individuals for offering up their skills, expertise, and thoughtful review: Peter Bogardus, Mary Hamilton and Emma Ferguson of Davis LLP; Joanne Taylor from the Nidus Registry; Eric Feilden of Cinnamon Jang Willoughby; Lauri Thompson, Doug Brodhead, Pat Tesan, Ted Kuntz, and Susan Whittaker from PLAN.

Without Dave Driscoll at the VanCity Community Foundation together with the Law Foundation of British Columbia, the first edition of *Safe and Secure* would never have been published. Thank you for your original grants.

While not directly associated with the production of this book, I would like to acknowledge the long-term support and confidence placed in our work by Faye Wightman and the Vancouver Foundation and Tim Brodhead and the JW McConnell Family Foundation. They have provided us with the resources and confidence to keep PLAN strong and continuously innovative.

Thanks to Kris Klaasen and Teresa Gustafson from Working Design. Your design and production values are as elegant as they were on the first edition.

To Alexis Pidlisecky, who has kept PLAN functioning so smoothly for so long, thanks for lending your excellence and high standards to this edition and to our organization.

A special thank you to Linda McDaniel, our editor, coordinator, and trouble shooter. She has lived and breathed *Safe and Secure* through many editions and has made a better writer out of me.

Thanks to Jack Styan, PLAN's Executive Director, for contributing the RDSP content.

And finally, special thanks to my co-authors, Jack Collins, and Vickie Cammack. This book is a tribute to your leadership and inspiration.

Al Etmanski

Statement from Minister of Housing and Social Development

The BC Government is committed to building the best support system for people with disabilities and their families in Canada. Our communities are enriched by the participation and contribution of people with disabilities and we are committed to helping families develop solutions which best suit their needs.

The BC Government is also committed to making the new RDSP as useful as possible to individuals with disabilities and their families. As such, we were the first province to waive the asset limit and to permit use of funds from the RDSP without penalty. Further and in addition to making a copy of *Safe and Secure* RDSP Edition available to individuals and families throughout the province in partnership with the Vancouver Foundation and PLAN, the BC Government will contribute financially to 30,000 individual RDSP's for eligible British Columbians.

Safe and Secure offers helpful information related to disability benefits, taxation, trusts, Representation Agreements, wills, estate planning and, of course, the new RDSP. It also contains stories of individuals and families, documenting the courage of parents and the amazing transformation that occurs when a person is surrounded by caring friends and family members. I am confident that families will see themselves in these stories and the possibilities of a better future they offer to their relatives with disabilities.The BC Government is pleased to sponsor this special RDSP edition of *Safe and Secure*.

BRITISH
COLUMBIA
The Best Place on Earth

Sincerely,

Rich Coleman

Minister of Housing and Social Development

Preface to the RDSP Edition

For twenty years parents and other family members of a loved one with disabilities have grappled with some very tough questions: Who will take an interest in our family member, particularly after we are gone? Who will love them? Whom will they love? Who will protect and keep them safe? Who will appreciate and nurture their gifts?

The experience of thousands of families and caring friends that have come through the Planned Lifetime Advocacy Network (PLAN) over the years is the inspiration behind *Safe and Secure*. Although difficult questions continue to persist and our concerns today are the same as they were then, we are united in the belief that we can create a good life for our loved ones with disabilities. This is the essence of love.

The absence of clear answers to these and other questions led us to create a unique type of organization: one led by families and one with an independent financial base. PLAN specializes in assisting families in creating a good life for their relatives with disabilities.

For two decades, PLAN has focused on what is loveable about our family members rather than on what is "wrong" with them. That's because we are surrounded by people like you who are deeply in love. This includes moms and dads, naturally. Equally, it includes, sisters, brothers, aunts, uncles, grandparents, cousins, friends, neighbours, and in many cases, service providers, professionals, and government workers.

We are united by the common bonds of caring and affection for our sons, daughters, friends, and family members with disabilities and a common desire to ensure their safety and well-being.

This book is one vehicle for passing on our knowledge, for sharing our stories, for inspiring you to act, and for improving the life of your loved one. Plunge in. Start anywhere. We are confident the straightforward principles of *Safe and Secure* will provide you with peace of mind and the realization that you are not alone.

First written in 1996, this edition has been extensively revised and updated. The immediate catalyst was the availability of the Registered Disability Savings Plan, the first of its kind in the world. PLAN led the initiative to create the RDSP, proposing it and lobbying for it; researching its benefits; convening and mobilizing families; and engaging with the Federal Government of Canada to have it made into law. The RDSP is an important new resource for ensuring that people with disabilities do not have to live in poverty. This is especially true since the Government of British Columbia has recently made it easier for people with disabilities to accumulate savings without jeopardizing disability benefits.

We invite you to join a growing worldwide movement that is thinking about disability in a new way and initiating new actions. We share the certainty that every person with a disability makes unique and valuable contributions and that we all benefit when these contributions are given. As we take charge of the future—and as we nurture caring networks for people with disabilities—we are awakening the world to the ties that bind. When this happens, lives are transformed, communities are changed, and our capacity to care for one another is enhanced.

As you know, and as we continually discover, love has everything to do with it.

Al Etmanski
President and Co–founder of PLAN

Family is
who loves
you.
WAYSON CHOY

Contents

Love is not enough

There are at least two emotions that inspired you to pick up this book. The first is love. The second is fear. We know this because we experience them too, as do the hundreds of families who have relatives with disabilities we have met over the years. You are definitely not alone.

Like everyone else, you want to die with your affairs in order. You want to leave a clear blueprint of your wishes for your relatives. At a time of great emotional stress—your death—you want to minimize the trauma. You also want to provide a secure future for those who survive you, particularly your relative with a disability.

That's the voice of love speaking.

Nevertheless, over 50 per cent of Canadians die without a Will. Most of the other 50 per cent haven't had their Will reviewed and updated for at least five years. And surprisingly, over 90 per cent of all business owners in North America die without a viable estate plan.

That's the voice of fear speaking.

So let's get right down to it. In matters of future planning, love is not enough. That's one of the main reasons this book has been written. We want to do three things:

1. We want to inspire and challenge you:
   - to begin and complete the future planning process for your relative
   - to conquer your fears
   - to replace fear of the future with faith in the future.

2. We want to guide you through the process of creating a Personal Future Plan for your relative with a disability. We want to expand your vision of the possibilities and to help you put them into concrete terms.

> I don't think intelligence exists without love. Love is intelligence. What kind of intelligence would you have without love?
>
> ROBIN BLASER

3. Finally, we want to shed light on the legal/financial/technical solutions available to assist you to carry out your last wishes, and to share practical tips on how to apply these solutions to your unique circumstances.

What we believe

We believe in families. We believe in your initiative, your dedication, your creativity, your tenacity, and your commitment. We believe that your wishes, dreams, and desires for your relative can shape the future. We believe in a world of possibilities. We believe that if you are willing to commit to the process of future planning outlined in this workbook, then that is the future your relative will have.

This book allows you to look over the shoulders of other families who are on the same journey. In this workbook, you will meet people who are breathing life into their dreams right now and giving shape to a brighter future for themselves and for their relatives with disabilities. While the details of their plans may be different, the issues they are confronting are remarkably similar to yours.

Another belief of ours is that this book can help. It will provide you with an overview of the whole future planning process. There are no single answers, no single solutions, no miracles. In fact, some of the solutions will never look perfect. A Personal Future Plan is just a mixture of old-fashioned common sense, commitment, hard work, and a dash of bravado.

So enjoy, create, laugh, and cry.

Developing a Personal Future Plan – Six steps to a safe and secure future

Many of us never really take the time to sit down and discuss what our future intentions are for our relative with a disability. Nevertheless it does come up. Maybe it pops up when you are driving home from a family gathering. Maybe one of your children mentions something in passing, but the topic quickly changes. Maybe you wake up in the middle of the night and decide it's time to talk about it in the morning. But then you don't.

So many thoughts, ideas, worries, and concerns go rolling around in your head. You can hardly remember them all. How could you expect someone else to? There are so many confusing messages and countless pieces of advice, and so many complications. The need for resolution lurks just beneath the surface, emerging at the most unexpected times.

Sound familiar? That's our experience, too. Virtually all of the families we have worked with have encountered the seemingly overwhelming bits and pieces of advice and action required to prepare for the future.

Our work with families has convinced us that the process is not as complicated as it first appears. Further, we are convinced there are only a few key elements you need to focus on. We have combined these elements into what we call a Personal Future Plan. That is what this book is about. It is what we advise you to develop for your relative. But really, you will be developing it for yourself.

A Personal Future Plan is a six-step process families can follow to create a safe, secure and pleasant future for their relatives with disabilities. It includes the best of your experiences, your dreams and nightmares, your wishes for the future, and your knowledge and expertise. It combines all of these with the active involvement of your relative with a disability, other members of your family, and selected knowledgeable professionals.

It is a plan that you create, control, and direct. It is focused on the here and now. It is also geared to a time when you will no longer be around.

The six steps are as follows:

Step one	Clarifying your vision
Step two	Nurturing friendship
Step three	Creating a home
Step four	Making sound decisions
Step five	Achieving financial security
Step six	Securing your plan

A message for parents with younger children

As you will discover, there are a number of sections in the book specifically written for parents who have children under the age of 19. These include pages 96, 150, and 183.

How to use this book

We suggest you skim through this book until you come to a section you'd like to work on. Once you've decided to focus on one section, answer all the questions and complete all the worksheets. If you don't want to mark up the book—and most don't—you can download the worksheets from www.PLAN.ca. Click on *Safe and Secure* Worksheets. You'll be surprised how the questions in one section will lead directly into the concerns of another section. Each one informs and guides the other. Before you know it, your planning will be complete and you'll have a record of your intentions—all contained in one place.

This book allows you to be an informed consumer of the professional services that are available in the future planning industry. By following the steps and advice presented here, you will be better prepared, use less professional time, and save yourself money.

We invite you to customize this book to your needs. Add your own personal data, photos, records, medical information, and so on. Keep this book in a safe place. You should never underestimate how valuable this information will be to your survivors.

Think of it as your manuscript to the future.

clarifying your vision

I am a sailor in my dreams
I travel from land to land
My heart is a compass
I will never be lost.

LIZ ETMANSKI

Rick's chances were down to one

GEORGE HALL'S life is a paradox. Like that popular movie from some time ago, George has gone "back to the future."

"My wife and I always felt we should be independent with this problem," says George. "Yet seven months before she died my wife said, 'We still haven't done anything about Rick.'" George's story is a familiar one to parents raising children with disabilities.

"After Rick's birth, my wife and I, well mainly my wife, focused her time and energies raising Rick. There wasn't an infant development program then, you know. A bunch of us parents got together. We helped each other. We started a school for Rick and others like him in the basement of one of the local churches. Nothing fancy, mind you. And we raised the money to hire the teachers and buy the supplies. Eventually we got the government to take them over.

"I was involved in the local association for ten years. For a time I was on the provincial board as well.

"I remember back when someone proposed a Lifetime Friendship Plan. The idea was to pay for friends to look in on the disabled person after their parents died. You see, parents have always been concerned about their children's future. We used to talk about it all the time. What would happen if one or both of us were run over by a car? I used to phone the provincial association periodically to see if there were any new developments. There never were.

"Then my wife took ill and matters really came to a head. We had our Will prepared during that time and we arranged with a trust company to manage the money we left in Rick's trust.

"Still my wife kept saying, 'Isn't there something else we can do?'"

After George's wife died, he was devastated. "As you can imagine it was a terribly painful time. Normally I'm a pretty optimistic person but I confess there were days when my dreams for Rick turned into nightmares.

"I knew I had to do something. Somehow the plans my wife and I had put in place didn't seem adequate now that she was gone. I figured Rick's chances were down to one."

—

This haunted George. Finally, one chilly spring day, he made one of his periodic calls to the provincial association. This time they had an answer. They mentioned the Senior Parents Network led by Jack Collins and Vickie Cammack and suggested he might want to look into it. The Senior Parents Network initiated by the Family Support Institute was simply a group of parents in similar situations. Their common bond was their willingness to search for an answer to this question: "If we were to die tomorrow, what would happen to our relative with a disability?"

George found an instant solidarity with these parents. Their worries were the same as his. Their questions were no different from the ones on his mind.

continued on page 20

step one
Clarifying your vision

Remember the old saying: If you don't know where you are going, any road will get you there? Well, we think it's true. That's why, as you begin planning for the future, you need to be clear about what you want. What are you trying to achieve for your relative? What do you imagine for their future? What are your goals? What do you want to prevent? To maintain? What do you want people to know when they gather to discuss your wishes after you are gone?

Without specific answers to these questions, the rest of your planning will be cloudy and incomplete. Knowing what you want to achieve is the first step in creating a Personal Future Plan.

For most of us, the obvious place to start is by completing our Will and establishing a trust for our relative.

Most of the planning time should be spent identifying what you are trying to achieve, thinking through your goals and objectives, and clarifying your vision. Once these steps become clear, you will be in a better position to evaluate the various options available. Then the technical solutions such as increasing the value of your estate, choosing your trustee, and finding the precise legal clauses will follow. Then— and only then—should you seek the advice of professionals. Your will and estate plan will be more relevant and useful because your directions are clear.

Think of your last plane ride. Did you ask the pilot where you should go? Of course not. You made that decision first. Then you examined the scheduling options and made your decision about price and so on. That's the most effective way to utilize the services of will and estate planning professionals. It saves them time and you money.

George liked their honesty. He enjoyed their humour. Parents helping parents.

That motivation led this group of senior parents to mount an international search to discover how parents elsewhere were confronting the challenge of creating a secure future for people with disabilities. They collected material from Canada, United States, Australia, New Zealand, and England.

George and the others took the best of what existed elsewhere and spent the next five years developing a new organization which eventually became PLAN.

George was so impressed by the thoroughness of the review that he became a founding board member of PLAN. He agreed with the philosophy: self-sufficiency through member contributions, entrepreneurial fund-raising, and independence from government. As parents who had been promised many miracles during the life of their child with a disability, they were careful not to promise any miracles.

They had two assets. One was their wisdom. They liked to joke that their past mistakes had created enough scar tissue to make them clever. Now they had good instincts. They could smell the mistakes coming. Their second asset was the interest and enthusiasm of a younger generation of parents. By this time the Senior Parents Network had become a full-fledged, parent run, non-profit charitable society called PLAN.

Today PLAN welcomes individuals of all ages and families of every configuration regardless of condition, illness or disability. One of George's peers fondly describes PLAN as the only "condition notwithstanding" organization she knows. George is equally proud that PLAN has become a vehicle big enough for anyone concerned about the future of individuals with a disability.

"We have so much in common. PLAN has provided us with a marvelous opportunity to work together. With that amount of energy, wisdom and talent, no one can stop us." ∎

What is a personal future plan?

A Personal Future Plan is a written summary of your plans for the social and financial well-being of your family member with a disability.

We have learned that the most effective question when making a Personal Future Plan is: What is a good life? Families tell us that a good life for their relative should include the following elements:

- caring and loving relationships
- a place of your own
- choice
- contribution
- financial security.

The worksheets at the end of each chapter will assist you with answering this question for your family's unique circumstances. To download a copy, please visit www.plan.ca and click on the *Safe and Secure* Worksheets.

What is a vision?

The fundamental job of the imagination in ordinary life is to produce out of the society we have to live in, a vision of the society we want to live in.

NORTHROP FRYE

Visions are creations of the heart as well as well as of the mind. A vision is your description of a desired future for your relative. A vision is about passion—your passion for the future economic and social well-being of your relative. That's why it is so important to address dreams as well as nightmares. Fears, worries, hopes, and dreams are all keys to unlocked passion.

A clear written statement of your vision will help focus your attention. Since a vision reflects your values, your traditions, and your family history, it creates a context for the other components of your Personal Future Plan.

Clarifying and sharing your vision of a desired future for your relative:

- enables you to see the world through your relative's eyes
- invites the involvement of other members of the family
- encourages others to better understand what is involved and gets them thinking as to how they can help
- brings preferred and desirable scenarios into the open
- suggests new opportunities
- moves you forward
- changes the present.

If music be the food of love, play on

GARLAND COHEN was in her eighties when she and her son David joined PLAN. She had been pushing the future to the back of her mind for a long time, hoping for a miracle. Garland wasn't afraid of dying; she was afraid of leaving David alone.

David had an apartment in the basement of the house where he and his mother lived for 20 years. While he knew many people in the community, none of them knew one another. Garland's health was failing and she feared that David was growing increasingly isolated and might slip through the cracks.

With the help of PLAN, Garland set up a trust and started a network for David. Soon after, she was diagnosed with cancer. David's network provided the support she needed to die at home. After she passed away, the network helped David move into an apartment of his own.

In the years since Garland's death, David has said that the network gave him a sense of security about living in the community, and that he didn't feel alone. Over time, the network helped him tackle issues like employment, using computers, and going back to school. "They're very wonderful people," he said of his friends, and they said the same about him. John Meyer, an early network member and advisor to Garland in setting up a trust for David more than 12 years ago, observed that if Garland could see how David has thrived, "She'd be tickled pink."

•

At the age of 61, when David was diagnosed with brain cancer, his friends rallied round. Weeks later, on a December evening, he and more than 75 others gathered in a room filled with Christmas cheer to celebrate his extraordinary life.

David's dedicated patronage of the musical arts was evident among the guests. Canada's first lady of opera, Judith Forst, related how, for decades, David had been coming back stage after every performance to compliment her. "When David loves something," she said, "it isn't 50 percent, it's 100 percent." Linda Lee Thomas, lead pianist with the Vancouver Symphony Orchestra, said, "A concert of the VSO is not complete without David Cohen. He comes back stage and always has that wonderful hand extended and shares his generous thanks."

David was also well known in political circles. He inherited his mother's passion for peace and social justice, and his letter writing for Amnesty International is legendary. During civic elections, David volunteered for COPE and later Vision Vancouver, and he rarely missed a local political meeting. At the party for David, Vancouver mayoral candidate Jim Green—out of the country at the time—sent a letter recalling how David's presentation on a panel about the opera, Of Mice and Men, moved a tenor in attendance to tears.

Others spoke of David's kindness, the thoughtful way he thanks people, and his generous spirit. Lyle Lexier, a member of David's

continued on page 24

We have learned that sharing your ideas—particularly when you put them in writing—is important. Since you won't be around, it is better to begin the discussion with your other children, extended family, friends, and potential supporters now. Relying on others without telling them could create problems for everyone.

You don't want to assume—as one Mom we know did—that her other children know and understand the complete medical background of her son, only to find that they were too busy growing up to notice, let alone to make notes! Or a Dad who told us that he intends to rely on his next-door neighbours to carry out his wishes for his daughter, without determining first whether they are interested in discussing any of the details with him!

So what are we afraid of?

What keeps so many of us from even thinking about the future let alone formalizing our future wishes for our survivors? What causes our paralysis? Why don't we act? Maybe it's fear.

Love and fear are two sides of the same coin. The coin is called passion. The word, passion, stems from the Greek and Latin words for suffering. Wouldn't you agree that suffering is a mixture of love and fear?

Fear is an intriguing emotion. Fear distorts our perception and confuses us about what is going on and about what is possible. When we use words like can't, ought to, if only, doubt, and impossible, we are under the influence of fear. Fear draws a dark and cold curtain between our intentions and our actions. Like a schoolyard bully, its appearance is deceiving. It's actually more imposing in our minds than in reality.

In our own personal struggles with the issues of future planning and in our work with families, we can identify three schoolyard bullies that everyone must find the courage to confront. We offer them here because we believe that where there is clarity, there is comfort. Where there is understanding, there is the ability to change.

FEAR OF OPENING UP Sharing your hopes and worries means discussing intensely personal matters with others—our spouse, family

If music be...

continued from page 22

network, said, "David Cohen has been my friend for 15 years. We talk about opera and human rights and the release of political prisoners and how to end capital punishment." Longtime friend Owen Underhill disclosed, "I don't think I've ever felt so affirmed in my life as when David left me a telephone message about my work as a composer, a conductor, a father, and a friend."

Network member Barrie Vickers spoke for everyone in the room when he addressed the guest of honour, "It is a wonderful gift you have given us David, and we'll live out the joy that you've given to us."

When David took the microphone, he said, "Thank you for your beautiful words." Then the whole room joined in a rousing verse of Hark the Herald Angels Sing. A long line formed at David's side, and for the next hour he graciously greeted friend after friend.

Sandra Shields

Post Script

David Cohen passed away peacefully and surrounded by friends on Friday, January 27, 2006. Some of his friends smile in relating how very fitting that the end of David's life should fall on Mozart's birthday—amid magnificent musical tributes. PLAN staff shall miss David's daily phone calls that kept everyone up to date on current events and local performing arts schedules. As one of the people on David's network remarked, "He had a good life and a good ending. Really, what more could anyone ask for?"

members, friends or acquaintances, and professionals. This may be awkward. We may need to contact people who have never demonstrated any interest in our relative. Or we may not know who to turn to or who to trust. And we risk rejection.

We've grown up believing in self-sufficiency. We've taken our responsibilities seriously. We've tried all our lives to make sure others wouldn't have to shoulder our responsibilities. We've done the best we can.

With future planning we have to share our hopes, our dreams, our fears, and our anxieties with others. We need to ask others to:

• help us with our planning
• carry out our wishes after we are gone
• believe in our relative and the possibilities for their future.

To do this, we need to reach out. We need to know who we can rely on. After all, what good are your plans if no one else knows about them? Sure, they could read about your wishes in your Will. But will the readers get the complete picture? Will they know what you really want? What if they have questions? Maybe they aren't interested? How can you be sure you will be understood?

FEAR OF DEATH Death is not a popular topic in our society. Even a cursory look at the popular media suggests that our culture is obsessed with youth, living forever, and avoiding sickness and infirmity. An illusion is offered: We can cheat death. While it may not be stated, the implicit message is that diet, exercise, and medical intervention will keep us forever young or forever alive. As Margaret Mead said of our culture, "When people are born we rejoice, and when they're married we celebrate, but when they die we try to pretend nothing has happened."

The fear of death is there for all of us. It lurks just beneath the surface, never quite deep enough, though, to be ignored. Perhaps it presents itself as anxiety, perhaps as an awful sense of impermanence, perhaps as loneliness. We may harbour the belief that parents who have sons and daughters without disabilities have fewer anxieties about death than we do. Not true. Perhaps what separates us from those parents is our need to address the future of our relatives not just for our lifetime, but for their lifetime.

For younger people, death can feel very remote. Even thinking about it seems perverse. But death is inevitable and is a natural part of life which we all have to face sooner or later. The Dalai Lama says there are two ways we can choose to deal with the prospect of our death: we can ignore it or we can confront it. Confronting and accepting our own mortality spurs us into action. We gain the wisdom to accept the inevitable and the knowledge to realize that it's better for everyone if we think about—and as importantly—begin to organize our affairs.

> Statistically, 100% of the shots you don't take don't go in.
>
> WAYNE GRETZKY

FEAR OF MAKING A MISTAKE, OR FEAR OF NOT BEING PERFECT

Now here's an irony for you. In thinking about the future, many of us feel we need to create the "perfect" plan. We are afraid that we haven't covered all the bases. Somehow we think we can make the future perfect even though the day-to-day doesn't always turn out the way we planned.

According to financial and estate planners, lawyers, accountants, and everyone else involved in the future planning business, the most common excuse for not making a Will is the fear of not getting it right. Indecision can paralyze even those with the best intentions. In trying

Our own collection of top ten reasons for NOT preparing for your future

1. The future is uncertain. Better eat dessert first. SARAH LEE
2. I'm afraid that if I make a Will, I will die. JOE AVERAGE
3. I never think of the future. It comes soon enough. EINSTEIN
4. I'm not afraid to die. I just don't want to be there when it happens. WOODY ALLEN
5. I don't see any dark clouds on the horizon. There's nothing to worry about. GENERAL CUSTER, U.S. CAVALRY
6. I've developed a new philosophy—I only dread one day at a time. CHARLES M. SCHULZ, PEANUTS
7. Dying is a very dull and dreary affair. I intend to have nothing to do with it. SOMERSET MAUGHAM
8. The future is not what it used to be. PAUL VALERY
9. I have seen the future and it doesn't work. ROBERT FULFORD
10. The future is made of the same stuff as the present. SIMONE WEIL

Thoughts on putting it off

- We're not in crisis yet. We've still got lots of time.
- The process is too costly, both financially and emotionally.
- I don't know who to turn to. My community of support is too small.
- I'm worn out from too many previous battles. I just need a break.
- We're still young.
- The future is too hard to contemplate.
- I'm a procrastinator. I have a reputation to live up to.

to make perfect decisions, we risk indefinite delay. Perfection equals postponement. Doing our best is as perfect as it will ever get.

Plans evolve

Future plans will change as circumstances change. It takes time for your dreams to evolve. You can always update and revise your future plan. In fact, you should expect to make changes along the way. We all get wiser as we get older don't we? You can expect to gain insight and pick up tips.

Who among us can predict the future? Can we anticipate all eventualities? Here's a simple exercise: Place yourself twenty years in the past. Would you have predicted the destruction of the Berlin Wall? Barack Obama as President of the United States? The threat of global warming? The careers of your children? The size of your nest egg?

To put it another way: Have you ever made a decision without having all the answers? Would Columbus have set sail? Would Mother Theresa have moved to the slums of Calcutta? The truth is that we often have to proceed as best we can without all the answers. Hindsight is the only guarantee of perfect vision. ■

Reflections on having a personal future plan

- It's fair to other family members. They now know what's going on.
- My worries about outside interference are gone.
- I'm better prepared to face the unknown.
- I've done the best I can.
- I've left a legacy of love.
- I'm at peace.

Worksheet 1

After you're gone: clarifying your vision

It's the day after your death. Describe what a safe and secure life will look like for your relative.

_____

List ten words to describe a typical day for your relative, in the best of all possible worlds.

_____

Use some key words to describe your worst nightmare for your relative after you're gone.

_____

What is the most important message you want to leave your relative with a disability? _____

_____

What do you want your survivors to help with after you've gone? _____

_____

When your executors/trustees meet, what do you want them to do first? _____

_____

What are the three priorities you want future caregivers to remember about your relative?

1. _____

2. _____

3. _____

What are the important arrangements you've made to ensure a good life for your relative?_____

_____

How do you want to be remembered by your relative? _____

_____

Worksheet 2

A family portrait

Use this worksheet to develop a portrait of your relative as it will be an important record to pass on to your survivors.

Health

List names of current doctors, specialists, and health practitioners: _____

_____

List current health concerns: _____

_____

List current health treatments: _____

_____

List current health precautions and alternatives: _____

_____

Briefly describe key features of medical history:_____

_____

Education and work

List current educational and/or work activity: _____

_____

What are their future dreams in this area? What other possibilities would they like to explore?

_____

What are some highlights from your relative's school experience? What did they like about it?
What didn't they like about it? _____

_____

Who are the people from the past that your relative had or still has a close connection with?

_____

What are some highlights of your relative's work experience? What did they like about it? What
didn't they like about it? _____

_____

Housing

Describe current living arrangements:_____

_____

What are some future housing options/possibilities for your relative? _____

_____

Summarize previous living arrangements: _____

_____

What did your relative like about them, dislike about them? _____

_____

Who are the people who had a significant relationship with your relative in these previous living

arrangements?_____

_____

Leisure and recreation

List current social, recreational, cultural, artistic, and athletic activities: _____

_____

What are your relative's interests and preferred activities in these areas?_____

_____

What are some future possibilities in the area of leisure and recreation?_____

_____

What does your relative most like to do? _____

_____

Personal

How would you describe your family's beliefs and values? _____

_____

What customs and traditions are important in your family? _____

_____

Is spiritual and religious worship important for your relative? Is this an area that could be

explored further?_____

_____

What are the significant events, markers or milestones in your relative's life? _____

_____

What brings comfort and peace to your relative?_____

_____

Who has been your relative's greatest source of emotional support?_____

_____

What does your relative gain the most pleasure from? _____

_____

Who are the most significant people in their life? _____

_____

What are their favourite possessions? _____

_____

Worksheet 3

A letter to the future

The last wishes of family members are honoured and respected in our society. A letter to the future is your opportunity to tell your survivors how you would like to be remembered, and how you would like your relative with a disability to be cared for.

   This is not an easy letter to write. Think of it as the letter you might write in the middle of the night when you can't sleep. Be frank about your hopes and fears. Tell those who will survive you what's most important to you.

Dear _____,

With love,

nurturing friendship

We spend our free time with friends. We can relax with them and allow our masks to fall. It is all right to be ourselves and we can do what we like, we are not constrained by rules.

But friendship also implies commitment. A true friend feels responsible for his friends, during bad times as well as good, in success and failure, humiliation and sorrow.

JEAN VANIER

A web of support for Rick

"I'VE SEEN A LOT OF PROGRAMS come and go. Many of them are baloney—no matter how thin you slice it! At one of these senior parent meetings, this young woman came around and started talking about circles—circles of friends. Well, I have to admit I thought it was one of those baloney stories. How could this possibly work?

"It was too theoretical. It looked good on paper but it would never work.

"But they turned the tables on me. They said they wanted a guinea pig for one of those circle things. I guess they figured if they could convince me they could convince anyone. Several of the other parents were prepared to take the risk. So I took a chance. Remembering what my wife had asked I said to myself, 'What have I got to lose?'

"Now, at the time Rick knew only a couple of people. He had a very narrow social life. He bowled once a week. And he attended a program at the community centre. That was it. He wasn't working or in any kind of a day program although he used to work at Campbell Industries."

When George came home to talk to Rick about the circle, he got a chilly reception. In fact, Rick was downright cold to the idea. Rick was emphatic.

"Do what you want. Just don't include me!" said Rick.

Not a great start.

George explains Rick's disinterest simply. "Rick had been to many services over the years and attended lots of classes and nothing ever changed for him. I guess I really couldn't blame him. I felt the same way."

Despite his own ambivalence, George persevered. To this day he doesn't really know why. Perhaps it was the memory of his wife's insistence to do more. Perhaps it was his apprehension about the future—he was ready to try anything. Perhaps it was because other parents were also trying it.

George had other anxieties. He and his wife had never discussed their concerns about Rick's future with any of their relatives. It was a private matter. It was their responsibility and theirs alone. Would they be interested? Wouldn't they be too busy? Did they even like Rick?

George didn't know it at the time but this is the hardest part for most families—asking family and friends for help.

"It was the most awkward part of it," he admits. "You feel so exposed. You're brought up to take care of your own. Asking for help was just not in our vocabulary."

Finally he hit upon a solution. PLAN had developed a short questionnaire mapping the relationships in the life of a person with a disability.

continued on page 40

Nurturing friendship

There is probably no one who can ever look after your relative with the same persistence, interest, and determination as you do. That's a fact. However, unless you've tapped into the fountain of youth, you won't be around forever. That's a fact, too. So what's the next best thing? The best guarantee of a safe and secure future for a person with a disability is the number of caring and committed friends, family members, acquaintances, and supporters actively involved in their life. It's as simple as that.

Friends make gifts and gifts make friends.

INUIT PROVERB

The real strength of these caring relationships comes not just in their connection to the person with a disability but in their connections with each other. Imagine a spider's web. The strands extend from the centre of the web to the edge. Imagine if there was nothing else holding them together. They would flap in the wind. Their functional value would be minimal. They need to be linked with each other in order to form the web. Otherwise spiders would starve! The strength of the web comes when all components are interconnected.

It's the same for our family members. The focus of support for people with disabilities must be placed both on their individual relation-

Worksheet 4 – The Web of Friendship

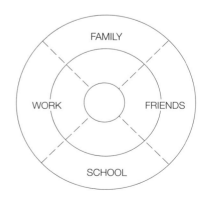

On pages 52 and 54, we've provided a sample web and a web for you to work with. To fill out your own web, follow the instructions on page 53.

The web will help you examine the current relationships in your relative's life and to explore ways of strengthening the network of support.

george's story
continued from page 38

George found the questions quite thought-provoking. He decided to mail the questionnaire out to his relatives to test their interest.

Some of them came to the first meeting, as did a neighbour and a former staff person of Rick's.

"Anyway, so there we were, all of us sitting around the room talking about Rick. There were eight of us at the first meeting. Rick was in the other room, but his name kept coming up. I guess he was straining to listen. Pretty soon he was standing at the entrance to the living room. Before you knew it he was sitting down with the rest of us and joining in the conversation. That was a turning point for Rick and me. Neither of us could believe that people were actually interested in him that way.

"After the circle formed, Rick went through a change. He had always been very quiet—a bit of a loner. Either keeping to himself or doing things just with me. He was never one to initiate a conversation, never one to pick up the phone. Soon he found there were people he could talk to. And they would phone him. And they'd go for coffee or something. And he was phoning them!

"You know it all adds up. Rick gets all kinds of help now, beyond our wildest imagination. In fact, I couldn't have imagined any of this five years ago."

For George that has been the greatest benefit of the circle. He can sit back and watch a web of support being spun for Rick before his eyes. It's almost like watching a movie about the future from the comfort of your easy chair.

George is confident that Rick's network isn't going to evaporate. He knows it doesn't depend solely on his input anymore. It will carry on without him. ∎

ships and the relationships among the members of the personal network. These interconnections create the web of support that begins to approximate the thoroughness with which families care for each other. PLAN's specialty is facilitating these caring relationships for people with disabilities. We call them Personal Networks.

A Personal Network is a team. People who come together for three basic purposes: the safety, health, and well-being of your relative, the person at the centre of the network. A healthy Personal Network is one where all members are in touch with each other, coordinating their involvement, and staying on top of things. They are united by bonds of friendship, love, and trust. This is the sum of everything you embody but won't be able to provide forever.

The role of friendship in our lives

The oldest literature from all cultural traditions attests to the importance of friendship. Themes about our interconnectedness are but one indication that we are, above all else, social beings. Friendship is a necessity for all of us, as important and essential to life as food and drink.

Aristotle, a Greek philosopher and major influence on Western thought, put it succinctly: "For without friends no one would choose to live, though he had all other goods." Perhaps it's because friendship is so fundamental to our existence that we take it for granted... or we aren't conscious of its importance until it is brought to our attention.

A recent Canadian political leader's comment on his recovery from a life-threatening illness underscores this point. Aside from the centrality of his wife and children to his thoughts, he observed that much of his time during recuperation was spent counting the blessings of friendship. In particular, he recalled those friendships that had lapsed or had been fractured and his determination to repair them.

When asked to boil our life down to its basics, most of us would agree that we are *interdependent* not independent beings. The impact of this recognition is far greater than our contemporary society appreciates or acknowledges. Understanding this interdependence is

- People with supportive social ties are less likely to become ill.
- Social contact helps us to heal more quickly.
- Social supports affect the sense of control we have over our well-being and improve our ability to stick with healthy behaviour patterns.

critical to our health, our quality of life, our sense of belonging, our peace of mind, and our security. And, therefore, it is also fundamental to the future security of our family members with disabilities.

The foundation of this future security is not the size of the estate you leave or whether you have a Will. Yes, these are important factors in building a successful future plan. But they are not enough. We agree with Emily Dickinson who wrote, "my friends are my estate." What provides texture and vitality and makes all living worthwhile are caring relationships and friends.

Friendships—ranging from acquaintances to intimate relationships—are formed by choice. They are freely given, based on mutual interests. Friendships are not one-sided. They are reciprocal, a two-way exchange. They are not paid visitors. They are not volunteers. They are not one-to-one workers.

Good friends support us through good times and bad, when we are on our best behaviour, and when we are not. We don't change ourselves to be with friends. Our gifts and our frailties are accepted as part of who we are. Our friends are not expected to fix us. They are just there. Friendships are naturally enjoyable.

When we are truly loved and valued, we gain a sense of belonging. When we feel like we belong, we change for the better. Our confidence improves as does our self-esteem, our sense of well-being, and our quality of life. Life takes on new meaning. At PLAN, we have consistently witnessed this transformation.

Caring Relationships: a source of support

Think of our own lives. When someone close to us dies, we are not left alone. We still have supportive friends and family. We want this same caring, secure environment for our family member with a disability when we die. This means formalizing the existing relationships of our loved one into a Personal Network or creating a new Personal Network around them. It is the only answer to the question, "Who will replace you when you are gone?" Personal Networks can become the next best thing. Personal Networks can become your eyes and ears, arms and legs. Nothing offers peace of mind better than that.

The good feelings that arise from our connectedness to others are an obvious benefit of friendship. However, these good feelings are just the beginning in evaluating the benefits of caring relationships. Investing in an extended network of friends and family for our relative provides both short-term and long-term returns.

When it is time to monitor and advocate, our relatives with disabilities will benefit from the presence of friends and supporters. Individuals who lack supportive ties are vulnerable to a wide variety of negative consequences. If not surrounded by people who have a vested interest in their well-being, our relatives may be at risk for abuse, neglect, and exploitation. Further, the needs of our relatives can be ignored by a busy, overworked service system unless friends are present.

Success in school and on the job is directly correlated with the size and health of our social networks. Social networks are also a determinant of health. There is now a mass of evidence to indicate that

Reciprocity

Personal Network members often describe how meaningful their relationship is with the person at the centre of the network. They talk about getting as much as they give. This is called reciprocity.

A few years back, we commissioned a study to document the experiences of Personal Network members. The results were impressive and confirmed our belief: people with disabilities make a real difference in the lives of Network Members. We also confirmed that the relationships between people with disabilities and Network Members were mutual. In the context of relationships, our family members are contributors.

social ties may be one of the critical factors distinguishing those who remain healthy from those who fall ill. Did you know that the health risks of being isolated are as detrimental as cigarette smoking? Clearly, friendships are necessary for good health.

The power and potential of Personal Networks have far exceeded our expectations. Over the past 20 years, we have seen members of PLAN's Personal Networks:

- monitor the formal programs and services that our relatives receive
- become effective advocates
- serve as executors and trustees or as advisors
- act as supportive decision makers and members of Representative Agreements (see Step Four)
- respond promptly and effectively to crisis
- solve problems and handle the unexpected
- carry out the wishes of parents.

Stages of a personal network

PLAN hires a Community Connector, who works an average of two to six hours per month, to create and nurture its networks. Vickie Cammack, President of PLAN Institute and a co-author of this book, developed this program. She advises that Community Connectors should "do as much as necessary and as little as possible."

Personal Networks take time, sometimes as long as one to two years before they have legs, as Vickie describes it. Or until the network members develop a close and tight caring relationship with each other and with the person at the centre.

Personal Networks go through three stages:

STAGE ONE: EXPLORATION This is the time for the individual, family, and the Community Connector to get to know each other; it's the time to focus on interests, passions, and possibilities for meeting others. At the end of this period, the Community Connector will provide a set of objectives, a time line of activities, and a list of potential network members.

STAGE TWO: DEVELOPMENT This is the time when all the leads and possibilities are followed up, contacts are made, and invitations extended. The goal in this stage is to recruit network members and to introduce them to each other. Practical strategies are developed.

STAGE THREE: MAINTENANCE By this time caring relationships have formed and networks meet regularly. The network settles in for the long run. As new interests emerge—and they often do—new connections are made. The network gets stronger and becomes more dynamic.

The art of making friends

Did you know that over 50 per cent of the first attempts pre-schoolers make to join in a group with other children are rejected? They must keep trying before being accepted by their peers.

In other words, the first step in meeting another person is a learned skill that comes with practice. This is a skill that most of us take for granted and which developed more or less naturally for most of us. A psychologist, Dr. Michael Guralnick, has observed that children with disabilities often do not experience this trial and error process. He suggests that there are three skills which very young children develop while playing with each other:

1. They learn how to initiate contact with peers;
2. They learn how to maintain play. These are the skills we learn to keep the interaction or relationship going;

Qualities of Community Connectors

PLAN's talented Community Connectors share similar characteristics. They:

- recognize and nurture the capacities and gifts of everyone
- pay attention to detail
- are great event planners

- are creative, pragmatic, and reflective
- know their community and use their connections.

3. They learn conflict resolution. Inevitably in any caring relationship, we have to learn to negotiate, to share, and to compromise.

Friendships rarely develop by chance. We cultivate them as carefully as we nurture a job or a family, a talent or a hobby. Some of us may think that friendships happen naturally and that, if they don't occur, there is nothing we can do about it. Not true. There appears to be a certain skill set associated with initiating and developing our acquaintances and friendships.

The ability to make friends may have to be relearned for some people. As a result of an accident or injury, their friends may have drifted away and their social circle changed dramatically. They may have had limited opportunity for socializing as a result of institutional living. They may be surrounded by staff who don't recognize the importance of friendship or don't know how to facilitate it. They may have tried to make friends, were rebuffed, and then became discouraged from trying again. They may lack or have lost confidence. They may believe that no one would want to be their friend.

Because friendships do not always develop naturally for some of our family members with disabilities, it is often necessary to approach the development of caring relationships in a focused and strategic manner. PLAN hires a Community Connector to assist with developing and maintaining our Personal Networks.

What we've learned about personal networks

- They take time, about two years on average, to become a smoothly functioning team.
- It's important to focus on people's interests, passions and what they can do. There are enough people focusing on what they can't do.
- Connections among and between network members are as important as their relationship to the person at the centre.
- There are more people interested in developing a caring relationship with your relative than you may think!

Significant contributions

Personal Network members make significant contributions because they:

- see the gifts and abilities of our relatives
- validate our relatives by letting them know they are valued
- help our relatives develop their talents
- create opportunities for our relatives to make contributions.

How caring relationships challenge families

While many families recognize the importance of caring relationships in their relative's life, they often feel some ambivalence when it comes to actively seeking opportunities for these relationships to form. From our experience, there are three challenges that families face: asking, opening, and believing.

ASKING To ask is to make ourselves vulnerable. There is always the possibility of refusal. Yet reaching out and asking is integral to developing and deepening our relationships. Friendships often form because we ask others to participate in a shared activity. We invite acquaintances over for tea to get to know them better. We ask neighbours to help us with building a fence. We ask friends to give us a hand with setting up for a party. Each of these casual invitations presents an opportunity for the relationship to grow into a caring one.

This process is not as easy when it comes to reaching out on behalf of our family members. We grew up with the unwritten expectation not to complain and to take care of things ourselves. We are fiercely and justifiably proud of our self-sufficiency.

We may feel that extending even a casual invitation is risky. We worry that others will feel obliged—or worse—that they might be saying yes because they feel sorry for us or for our relative. This worry speaks to how deeply many of us have been hurt by negative cultural stereotypes about disability. It makes us forget the gifts our relative has to offer. It makes us forget that others may indeed care.

We need to remind ourselves of the beauty and richness our family member has added to our lives and to the lives of those around

I let go and trusted. We moved fast and wild. I had no idea what it looked like, nor did I care. The dancer inside me was out.

BONNIE SHERR KLEIN

them. We constantly hear stories from ordinary people attesting to how their relationship with our sons and daughters has brought meaning to their life. These are often people who wanted to reach out but did not know how. Each invitation we offer is an opportunity for others to extend their community and to broaden their relationships.

OPENING In order for others to come into our lives, there needs to be a place for them. It is impossible to meet people or deepen a friendship if we have no time to spend with them. This is an issue for many people with disabilities. Virtually all areas of their lives may be programmed. From an outsider's perspective, there is no apparent need for a friend. Our relative may be too scheduled for friends and acquaintances to spend time with them. We may need to give up a program or change schedules to create the space that would allow for others to engage with our relative.

On a more subtle level, some of our own actions might inhibit the involvement of others. Over the years we may have become used to doing many things for our family member. The presence of others changes our routines too. The involvement of somebody new might be threatening. Shouldn't we be doing it? That's good, old fashioned guilt talking. We can do it better. What if *they* do it better? What will they think of us? That's letting fear do the talking for us. As we feel ourselves losing some control, we may resist or undermine the contributions of others. We need to ask ourselves honestly and courageously what we are willing to let go of in order to make room for others to become active and involved in the lives of our relatives.

When you really think about it, this process of letting go is our lifetime task. It is why you are reading this book. Friendships provide a catalyst to accomplish this task. Our family members grow richer from having experiences outside of their immediate family. Their friends can inspire and encourage them to participate and contribute to society.

BELIEVING Of the three challenges, this may be the greatest. We worry that the distinctive traits or history of our loved ones may make them unloveable, to everyone, that is, but us. We remember the absence of invitations to birthday parties or sleepovers. We notice—

No disability precludes relationships.

VICKIE CAMMACK

This is a portrait of facilitated social network development across Canada. Author Nancy Rother describes the seven critical elements of resilient social networks, explores challenges, and offers practical tips. For more, please visit www.planinstitute.ca.

> The heart keeps looking for itself. It knows and does not know where it belongs.
>
> JAN ZWICKY

yet again—someone staring in the supermarket or we receive a look of pity from a passer-by. We feel hurt by these things and we ache for our relative. Our overwhelming desire is to protect, and we cannot find it in ourselves to truly believe there is a caring community of people available to befriend our loved one. This lack of belief affects our ability to be open to others, and to trust in their integrity.

After 20 years of nurturing Personal Networks at PLAN Canada—and in dozens of locations around the world—we can assure you, no disability can prevent a caring relationship from forming. No previous experience, no characteristic, no behaviour, not anything. And we don't just believe this, we know it. The proof is in the hundreds of friendships that have developed within our Personal Networks.

In spite of the negative view of an uncaring society profiled regularly in the media, people do reach out to each other. PLAN's experience bears this out. People are genuinely hospitable and eager to become part of our relative's life. Often they just need to be asked.

Our challenge as parents and families is to not let our fears dominate the opportunities for friendship.

Relationships and contribution

Relationships play an important role in enabling our sons and daughters to contribute their gifts. From the comfort of supportive friends, family, and Personal Network members, people with disabilities can find opportunities to work, volunteer, create, inspire, care, serve, and contribute.

Our family members make contributions in two ways:

CONTRIBUTIONS OF DOING These are the action-oriented contributions we are most familiar with such as volunteering and working.

CONTRIBUTIONS OF BEING These are contributions made by the majesty of our relative's presence. Being present is an important way for our family members to make their contribution. The exchange is fellowship and communion. Our relatives offer grace, caring, attentiveness, wonder, acceptance, silence, receptivity, compassion, inspiration, pleasure, gratitude, loyalty, and friendship. These gifts—often overlooked in our society—are critical to society's well-being. In fact, they are a necessary antidote to "too much doing."

Identifying the gifts and contributions of our relatives leads to meaningful relationships. See Worksheet 5 on page 55.

For more on the relationship between contribution and citizenship, see the discussion on the Philia dialogue on caring citizenship on page 181.

Tyze is an online service that works to create and maintain Personal Networks and is based on the proven PLAN network facilitation model.

Tyze is about the person at the centre of the network and the connections among the network members. It's a place to celebrate contributions and achievements; it's a way to stay connected to friends and loved ones. Please visit www.tyze.com.

Enough talk: the belonging initiative

There has been a lot of talk over the years about the importance of friendship for people with disabilities. Unfortunately there hasn't been a lot of action, until now that is.

A group of Canadian organizations has banded together to do something about ending isolation and loneliness. Members include L'Arche Canada, the Canadian Down Syndrome Society, Canadian Abilities Foundation, Canadian Association of Independent Living Centres, Inclusion Press, Developmental Disability Resource Centre, Laidlaw Foundation and, of course, PLAN and the PLAN Institute. For more information, please visit www.nurturingbelonging.ca.

That's what friends are for

There is something about being human that makes us yearn for the company of others, to be with and to be touched by our family and friends. Isolation and solitude are devastating by-products of having a disability. We believe that these by-products can be as much of a handicap as the disability itself.

Loneliness can weigh even heavier when a person with a disability is served by a large impersonal service delivery system which has little time or resources to focus on friendships. The only way to truly diminish this loneliness is by paying attention to caring relationships. Even though this may be challenging for both our family member and for us, it is critical for their future security and well-being.

The keys to creating these connections are first, our willingness to let them happen and second, our effort to make them happen. All the riches of the world will not compensate for the security of being cared about. That's what families do. That's what friends are for. ∎

Sample web

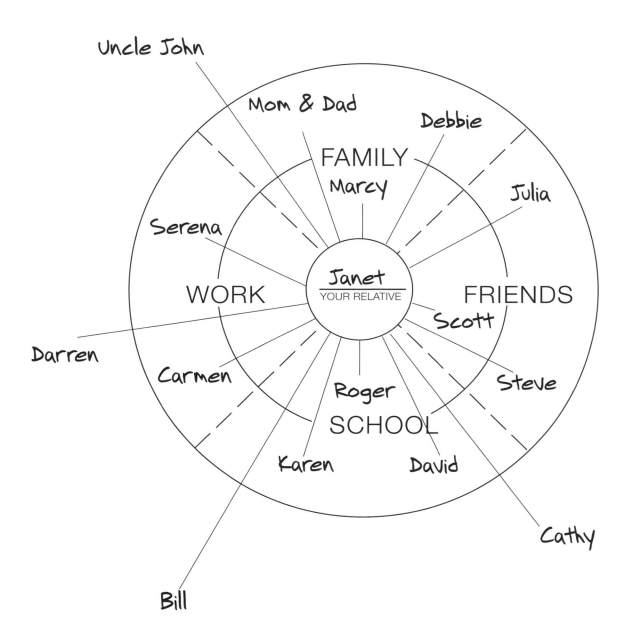

Worksheet 4

The Web of Friendship

The sample web has already been filled out. To fill out your own web:

1. Write your relative's name in the centre circle.

2. The inner circle represents the area in their life that is filled with people they trust, feel comfortable with, and confide in. They can be friends or family. However, exclude anyone in a paid position. The people in this circle will have a reciprocal relationship with your relative, based on friendship and respect.

3. The remainder of the web represents the rest of the people who are involved in your relative's life. Write their names down, using the distance from the centre to represent how close their relationship is.

4. If you wish, the dotted lines can be used to indicate the different areas in your relative's life. For example, family in the top section, friends on the left, school and work in the other quadrants. This will help you to visually demonstrate the interrelationships in your relative's life.

5. When you have completed this picture, think about how you can strengthen the web, by joining up the people in your relative's life. In a different coloured pen, draw in all the potential connections.

Your family member's web

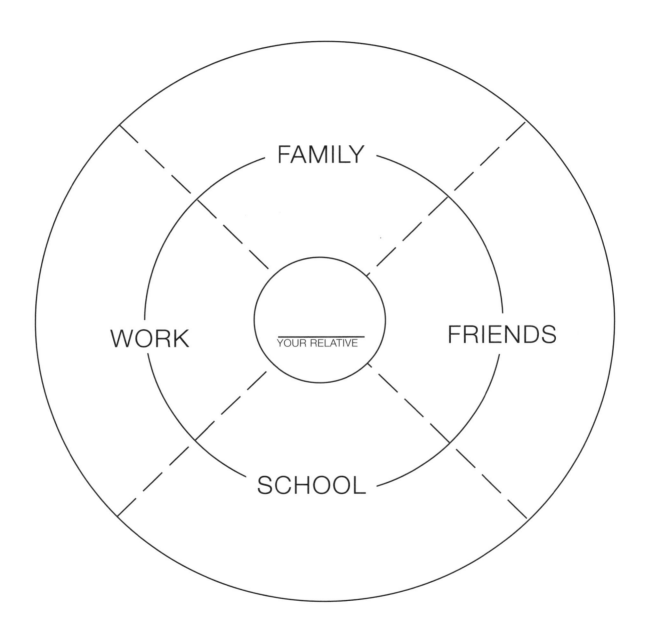

FAMILY

FRIENDS

WORK

YOUR RELATIVE

SCHOOL

Worksheet 5

Contribution

The following questions may help you identify the various ways your family member makes or could make a contribution.

    We suggest you answer these questions and then share with your family member and others who know them well.

What contribution does your loved one make to your family?

What are the three activities they love the most?

What are their passions?

What gives them the greatest joy and pleasure?

Who are their heroes?

What famous public personality (singer, actor, athlete) do they like?

What are their gifts of doing?

What are their gifts of being?

What would they like to learn?

What could they teach others?

What have you learned from them?

What positive attributes do others like about them?

What is the greatest accomplishment of their life so far?

What job or volunteer position would best suit their interests and personality?

creating a home

On a green island in Ontario
I learned about being human
built a house and found the woman
and we shall be there forever
building a house that is never finished

AL PURDY

Home alone too!

"MY WIFE AND I always expected that Rick would stay in our home. We thought perhaps the local community living association would take it over after we died, and turn it into a group home. Then Rick and others like him would live there.

"After attending a PLAN workshop on Letting Go, I began to wonder whether I was holding onto ideas that weren't in Rick's best interest. I had no idea if he would enjoy living with other people. I didn't know how he'd react to having staff supervising him. Well, actually I did know. Rick had lived in a group home years before and it hadn't worked out.

"Maybe I'm being a little stubborn here," I thought. Maybe it would not be best for Rick after all.

"I thought I'd better take this up with Rick. He didn't think too much of the idea at first. Then all of a sudden it was decided. Rick would move. Rick and his Personal Network decided, that is, not me. It was quite a shock."

Their neighbour across the street who had been invited to the first meeting knew of a vacancy in an apartment building that was centrally located. So Rick moved out. "It's a start," says George. "The apartment's his home now–he doesn't have his old man there to bother him.

"Fortunately there have been no big problems. He took it in his stride. Actually he has matured quite a bit as a result of the move. He likes to boast that he knows all 15 people in the building and they all talk to him. What a dif-ference from his old neighbourhood where so many of the people he knew had moved away. And I must admit I like the idea that he is surrounded by people who accept him and, in their own ways, check up on him."

And there's more. Rick has just found a two-bedroom apartment in the same building. Bob, his friend since childhood, is moving in with him. George suspects Rick has at least one more move ahead of him and that it will be into a place he owns himself, or at least a home that Rick's discretionary trust owns on his behalf. ∎

Creating a home

A home of one's own. This is the universal dream, occupying a powerful place in our individual and collective psyche. Home as haven and home as hospitality convey the intangible aspects of home. Home as feeling—the feeling you get when at the end of a long day you open your front door and exhale, Ah, I'm home.

In my book, *A Good Life*, I write about the essence of home having nothing to do with wood, nails, bricks, and mortar. Rather, it's about sweat and laughter, bruises and tears, stains and cobwebs, flowers and slammed doors, failures and promises, kisses and fingerprints. Home is where we can just be, where we become, where we belong. Home is not a program or a service; it is your haven and sanctuary.

The word, home, comes from a Sanskrit root meaning a safe place to lie down; a separation of outside from inside, defined by a threshold.

Isn't that the kind of place we want for our friends and family members with disabilities? A place that provides continuity and security? A place that ensures privacy and reflects the personality of those who live there?

> Only when you discover yourself can you be secure.
>
> DAPHNE ODJIG

Making a house a home

Parents the world over rank a stable and hospitable living environment as a high priority for their sons and daughters. A house, however, doesn't become a home by accident. It requires thoughtfulness and care. It starts by understanding the meaning of home to your loved one. What are they used to? How can you recreate that? How do you guarantee that a heap of living will take place there? See Worksheets 6 and 7 at the end of this step to help answer these questions.

Some of our sons and daughters will want to have their own place. They'll want to live on their own or with people they know and like.

The wisdom of mothers

THE WILL WAS CLEAR: sell my house. The executor was only following the instructions of Garland, David's mother. The home David had lived in for 28 years was to be sold. For a man who relied on order and predictability this could have been a disaster.

What was his mother thinking?

In fact she knew what she was doing. She was house rich and cash poor. All her money was tied up in her home. She needed to liquidate in order to finance David's trust and his financial security. Besides, she, PLAN, and David's Network had prepared for this time for two years.

Network Members helped David find his new place, an apartment in a stately old home in Kitsilano, right on the bus line. They borrowed a truck and helped him move. They built bookcases for his opera and classic movies video collection. They hung new curtains. Even the trust officer got into the act, collecting all the family photographs and placing them into the albums with David.

But the unthinkable did happen. On his first weekend in his new place David got locked out. He couldn't get in the main door. He tried and tried, becoming more and more frustrated. We imagined his mother must be turning in her grave.

Eventually David crossed the street to a phone booth and called one of his network members. No answer so he called another. John was home but lived on the North Shore—too far to get there quickly. John did, however, arrange for another Network Member to come right over.

Unable to make the keys work either, he invited David to spend the night at his home. The next morning they returned, spoke with the landlady who, it turns out, was the one who changed the lock. Turns out, David was not the only one having trouble.

David's mother had decided to rely on PLAN so she became a Lifetime Member. She realized she had no other choice since she was the last surviving family member.

She asked PLAN to provide advice to her trustee on expenditure from the trust and to keep David's network strong and vibrant.

Engaging three members of David's network after midnight and on a weekend isn't something she predicted but it is something she expected.∎

They'll need very little staff support. Others will be need intensive staff support.

Once this sense of home has been clarified, you can examine the type of tenure and other technical details that best suit your relative, and perhaps your pocket book! For example, at the end of this chapter—in Jackie's story—we will describe how the assets in an RDSP can be used to purchase a home.

Home can exist wherever you live and regardless of who owns or manages the building, house, apartment or room. The key to creating a home is to have control over the home environment; to make sure it reflects your family member's personality; to ensure that your family member chooses their own roommates. One of our past Presidents is very satisfied with the group home her son lives in and we have to say we agree with her. Every time she visits Peter there is laughter, surely one of the languages of home. Mind you, she is a respected advocate, who is on top of everything. She has briefed and prepared Peter's Personal Network to carry on her vigilance.

Regardless of where our relatives live we want them to have choice; in other words, we want our relatives to live in a place that respects their choices; a place where their personality shines through.

Many of us cannot afford to assist our family members in purchasing their own home. We're still paying down our own mortgages! There are alternatives to private home ownership, however, that will provide long-term stability. Housing cooperatives and land trusts, for example, have many of the advantages of home ownership. So does home sharing; that is, living with others who do not have a disability. If these options are not available or appropriate, we suggest you consider rental.

Rental accommodation—particularly rent to own—can allow people to establish a sense of their own place and to maintain control of their living environment. It may not be for everyone but being a tenant provides your relative with the flexibility to try different living arrangements, particularly when they are starting out and first leave home.

> If mealtime is a renewable resource, then food is a social lubricant that can keep the machinery of involvement and interaction running between people with and without disabilities.
>
> KAREN MELBERG SCHWIER
> AND
> ERIN SCHWIER STEWART

Going to my apartment now

ERIN IS LIVING IN A FULLY FURNISHED suite in the family home. The renovations were completed just before her parents left on a short vacation leaving Erin's friends and staff to begin the transition. In retrospect, the timing couldn't have been better.

On their return, they were met by Erin, her girlfriends, and a list. "We think Erin needs her own flat screen TV, not the 'old' one you gave her. And a docking station for her iPod. And speakers, of course."

"The suite has changed Erin's life, says Pat, and she's settled into her new place without any of the expected disruption."

The benefits of having your own place are not lost on Erin. While she may not articulate them, her communication is clear.

Although she eats dinner upstairs with the family she makes it pretty clear where she prefers to be. "Going to my apartment now," is an often-heard refrain. Pat's pretty sure it is not just to avoid the dishes. Erin's suite has become the hot spot in the house.

Staff and friends use Erin's entrance. Her status with her younger siblings has increased, especially with her younger brother. Parties seem to happen with regularity.

Recently Pat heard yet again the boisterous sounds of laughter in her daughter's suite. Heading downstairs she discovered a gathering of friends. After a polite length of time one of them came over to Pat and discreetly but pointedly observed, "I don't recall you being invited!"

This time Pat got it. If Erin's friends could take on her mother, they could take on anyone. ■

We see no reason why people who live in group homes and who need staff support for their personal care should be denied the benefits of living in a home-like setting. This may not be easy. Not every agency appreciates the difference between house and home. You may have to search for the right agency. You may have to advocate. You may have to change your relationship with the current service provider.

These options are more feasible now. The existence of microboards and the promotion of individualized planning and funding demonstrates a respect for the individual's wishes and a commitment to personalized, customized supports rather than catering to the needs of the group.

> I prefer grace to miracles.
> DAVIDE ROCHE

Limitations of current housing options

Governments spend millions of dollars every year on housing for people with disabilities. That's a good thing. The challenge for advocates and parents alike is to ensure that control of the home environment doesn't rest exclusively with the agency or service provider. The progressive agencies out there today are responsive and sensitive to making genuine homes out of their group living arrangements. But families still worry. What if there is a change in staff, the home supervisor, or in agency leadership? What will happen if there are funding cutbacks?

It's not that group homes, semi-independent living, and other residential options are wrong. But they do have their limitations. In our conversations and meetings with families, the following concerns about the current residential service system for people with disabilities surface repeatedly:

- there is no control over where their relative lives
- individual needs may be secondary to those of other roommates
- someone else decides who your family member lives with
- the personality of the home is often shaped by the people who work there, not by the people who live there

- some group homes may not welcome the involvement of family and friends
- there is no security of tenure
- families fear the loss of caring and understanding staff and home supervisors, as these types of changes have an immediate impact on their family members.

As a result, more and more families are looking for alternatives that provide flexibility, continuity, and greater control.

Home ownership

Home control means choosing:

- where you want to live
- with whom you will live
- the staff who will support you.

Homeowners have status in our society. The pride of ownership is one of our more important cultural values. Home ownership is the fulfillment of a dream even if we have a hefty mortgage and are borrowing money from a financial institution. Home ownership can also be a good investment, and a hedge against inflationary times.

Most of us take it for granted that we will own a home at some point in our lives. Until recently, this has not been the case for people with disabilities. In the past, it was a dream they and their families dared not consider. As our families members become more self-sufficient and as our plans to secure the future become more focused, home ownership for people with disabilities is becoming an option of interest. In fact, it is an option that more parents are exploring, more financial institutions are supporting, and governments are welcoming. Major home ownership initiatives are underway in Australia, the United Kingdom, and the United States. And more and more examples are being developed in British Columbia.

Whether the home is owned directly by your relative, owned jointly with you or others, or owned by their trust, for as long as they like your relative will have a choice in where they live, who they live with, and in the staff they hire. As one mother put it, "Roommates will come and go, support services will change, that's a given. But whether I am around or not, I know that the house—or I should say the home—will be there for my daughter."

Critical components of home ownership

As you might expect, making arrangements for home ownership for your family member can be complicated. The mix between financial and legal matters, health and safety concerns, and social support adds more considerations. It means paying attention to a number of critical components.

FINANCING THE PURCHASE Unless you are independently wealthy, this is a major challenge. The new Registered Disability Savings Plan (RDSP) provides families with a means to begin saving for the purchase of a home. The matching grants, the Disability Savings Bond, and compound interest will increase the size of the capital your relative will have available. We will explain the details of the RDSP in Step Five.

Other financing options used by families include:
- re-mortgaging the family home to access additional capital
- forming a partnership with other parents to purchase a home
- taking out a reverse mortgage
- working with local developers who, in return for zoning concessions from municipalities, will make affordable housing available
- earmarking part of their estate to establish a housing trust exclusively for the purpose of purchasing a home
- renting out the other bedrooms to help finance mortgage payments.

ASSISTANCE WITH RENOVATION The Canada Mortgage and Housing Corporation (CMHC) under two programs—the Residential Rehabilitation Assistance Program (RRAP) and the RRAP-D program—offers financial assistance to homeowners and landlords to improve their dwellings so they are more accessible to persons with disabilities. The amount you receive is based on the cost of mandatory repairs and the area in which you live. Currently, the maximum loan amounts range from $16,000 to $24,000. A certain amount of the loan may be forgivable, depending on income. Higher amounts of assistance may be available in more remote areas. For further information, contact CMHC of BC and the Yukon at 1-800-639-3938.

Home ownership means:

- control over where you live
- stability of tenure
- the opportunity to build up equity
- privacy
- a sense of place
- choice
- ability to offer hospitality
- security
- safety and comfort.

OWNERSHIP Here are some home ownership options you may want to consider for your relative:

- they have direct title
- they co-own the house with another person (for example, their spouse or a family member)
- you own the house together
- at least two families own the home
- your family member lives in a housing co-op that can build up equity
- your family member rents to own
- you arrange financing for your family member to live in a co-housing development. All financing (for each unit and the common areas) comes from the owners of all the units
- the house is owned by a trust in your family member's name (or by joint trusts if two or more people with disabilities are involved). The trust(s) can be established:
  - while you are alive; or
  - through your estate after your death.

TYPES OF CO-OWNERSHIP If more than one individual or family owns the home, you must choose one of these legal co-ownership options:

- joint tenancy; or
- tenancy in common.

HOUSING TYPES Just about anything is possible:

- single family
- condominium or row housing
- housing cooperative unit
- co-housing
- apartment
- mobile home
- infill housing (for example, converting a garage into a small housing unit)
- renovation of existing house
- purpose-built housing designed for your relative's needs; for example: shared kitchen, dining, and lounge areas.

Joint tenancy

Property owned jointly by two or more persons in which the surviving joint tenant(s) becomes the owner of the entire property when one of the joint tenants dies.

Tenancy in common

Property owned jointly by two or more people. Upon the death of one of the tenants-in-common, ownership of the deceased's shares is transferred to that person's estate, not to the other joint owner.

ONGOING MAINTENANCE If you purchase a house, you will need to make arrangements to cover:

The ongoing mortgage payments

- Will government income assistance be enough?

If not:

- When you are alive, will you supplement the mortgage payments out of a living trust, from family resources or from some other source such as the new RDSP?
- After your death, will the payments come out of a trust?

The major maintenance, repair and insurance costs as well as property taxes

- Will you pay for these costs yourself while you are alive or will you establish a living trust for this purpose?
- Will you establish a trust to cover these costs after your death?

NOTE: It is critical that you consult with a knowledgeable lawyer to establish the trusts referred to above. For example, you may want to ensure that you do not jeopardize your relative's entitlement to government benefits. BC disability assistance benefits have a housing cost component which is dependent on costs incurred. You may want to structure payments with this amount in mind.

The minor, ongoing maintenance

While this can be done by yourself in the short term, you may want to consider contracting with a property management company to provide this service. In addition, this may be a service you will need to request your trustee to provide. Obviously, if your relative lives in a condominium or a housing cooperative, property maintenance is already built into the housing agreement.

NEGOTIATING FUNDING FOR PROGRAM SUPPORT STAFF Unless you have the private means to pay for staffing supports, you will have to negotiate funding from government. Generally speaking, government is becoming more interested in supporting people to live in their own homes. After all, it represents a big savings if the capital costs of the home are not its responsibility. We suggest you use this argument when negotiating the supports necessary. You can argue that since you are financing the house, the government should finance staff supports.

SELECTING COMPATIBLE SUPPORT STAFF Not every staff person will be comfortable working in your family member's private home. Many staff will see it primarily as their workplace. We suggest you spend time clarifying in writing the values that are important to your relative. When hiring through an agency, become familiar with their operating philosophy. Interview their executive director. Visit some of their programs. Get to meet the people who receive services from them. Talk to their families.

Do not be afraid to let staff go if it appears they are not compatible with the values established for the home.

The future has already arrived. It's just not evenly distributed yet.

WILLIAM GIBSON

CHOOSING A COMPATIBLE ROOMMATE There is no scientific approach to this challenge. Some people are easy to get along with. Others are not. Often you won't know until you try. Many of the people who are now living in their own homes first tried living on their own in some form of rental accommodation. Then they invited someone to live with them. This is an excellent way to test the kinds of support you and your relative will need. It also enables people to have a better sense of who they want in a roommate.

TECHNICAL ADVICE FOR CONSTRUCTION AND RENOVATION We'll leave you to your own devices with this component. You will be able to access building contractors in your area far better than we will. Accessible building design advice is available from local disability resource groups if you would like additional expertise. Other parents are a good connection for families who are considering construction or renovation. Check our resource section for additional contacts.

Looking to the future

Times are changing. More people with disabilities are about to become home owners. They are gaining a measure of choice and control over their lives that they have never experienced before. When established with due respect and consideration for the issues identified here, home ownership also provides families with a concrete component of their plan for the future.

Families see themselves as part of the solution. With tax and trust concessions, more and more families will be willing and able to invest in the housing future of their relatives with disabilities and to partner with government.

This step—Creating a Home—connects with the other steps in this book. It does not exist in isolation. Without the existence of a network of personal support, our relatives will be just as isolated in their own place as anywhere else. Similarly, you will need to use your Will and trust agreement (see Step Five) to formalize the arrangements to own or rent as well as to make provisions for housing maintenance.

In addition, the next step—Making Sound Decisions—provides an overview on supported decision-making. This Step will assist you to protect your relative against exploitation in their home, to support their choices, and to monitor the home arrangements that have been made. ■

Everyone benefits when everyone belongs.

Examples of housing solutions

Given the complexity of issues and the unique circumstances of each individual and family, the following examples should serve only as illustrations of what is possible.

EXAMPLE ONE
Starting young: Jackie

Background

All Jackie wants to talk about is her last dance class, the time her choir got to go to Montreal, and the sleepover with her classmates at the Vancouver Aquarium. Grade 4 is a time of wonder and learning.

Don and Jasvir are more serious. Conversation reflects their concern for her security and continued happiness. "We take our choices for granted. Knowing that Jackie will have enough money to pursue her dreams is important to us," says Jasvir. They see the RDSP as a way of ensuring that she can make personal choices when deciding her future. They want her to be able go where she wants to go, to do what she wants to do, and to make choices that make her happy.

Don and Jasvir have discussed the RDSP and are planning to contribute $150 a month for the next 20 years. Jackie's grandparents also want to help. They've talked about contributing $25,000 to her RDSP at the start.

When Jackie is 39 years old, her RDSP will be an estimated $362,000. If she purchases a life annuity, she will have annual income in excess of $18,000 per year.

Another option is to use a lump sum from the plan to assist their daughter in purchasing her own home. If they withdraw $200,000 as a down payment when Jackie is 39, she can purchase an annuity that will pay approximately $8,000 per year for the rest of her life.

RDSP Summary:

Family taxable income: over $75,000

Annual family contribution: $150 a month ($1,800 a year)

Family contributions from age 9 to 28: $61,000 (including $25,000 from grandparents)

Value of Grant: $45,000

Value of Bond: $10,000

Investments: moderate risk (estimated return 5.5%)

Age to begin receiving from the plan: 39

Approximate value of the RDSP when payments begin (age 39): $362,000

Option A: No home purchase

Annuity payments: approximately $18,000 per year.

Option B: Home purchase at age 39

Withdrawal of $200,000 for down payment

Annuity payments: approximately $8,000 per year.

EXAMPLE TWO
Patricia, living in an apartment

Background

Patricia is a 38-year-old woman who lives on her own. After sharing a rental apartment with a friend for three years, Patricia moved into a housing cooperative where she stayed for two years.

Patricia's grandmother had left her a large sum of money which she had placed in a discretionary trust. John, Patricia's father, is trustee.

When Patricia decided to move out of the housing co-op, she and her dad decided to look for an apartment unit she could own. They found an affordable one-bedroom unit, centrally located near a large shopping centre, close to major bus routes and a short walk to the Skytrain.

Financing

The apartment unit cost $125,000.
Patricia's dad contributed $12,500 of his own money.
The discretionary trust contributed $97,500 in a no-interest second mortgage.
Patricia took out a first mortgage for $15,000.

Features

• Patricia has title to the apartment.

• Since her dad owns only a tenth of the apartment, Patricia is the principal owner. As homeowner she is eligible for the homeowner's grant. Also since this is her principal residence, the apartment is not subject to capital gains should it ever be sold.

• The fact that Patricia's father owns approximately a tenth of the apartment prevents a dishonest person from persuading Patricia to sell or to order major repairs.

• Should the apartment ever be sold, Patricia's father would get his money back and the amount of the second mortgage would be returned to the discretionary trust.

• The mortgage payments—plus hydro and maintenance costs—are equal to the shelter component of the BC disability assistance benefits Patricia receives.

EXAMPLE THREE
Thomas, staying in the family home

Background

Thomas is a 48-year-old man who currently lives with his parents. They want him to remain in the family home after they die. When that day arrives, the house will be placed in a trust for Thomas's continued use. To support Thomas, the family has arranged to establish two trusts (a residential trust and a family trust) and a micro board (see page 98).

Financing

The parents' estate plan provides for the home, including furnishings, to be left in a discretionary trust for the primary use and benefit of Thomas. The family calls this the "residential trust." The trust would have a small amount of funds to cover minor repairs.

A separate discretionary financial trust will provide additional assets to cover maintenance of the home, property taxes, extraordinary expenses, and the quality of Thomas's life. The family calls this the "family trust."

Community Living BC (CLBC) will be asked to contribute funding towards the daily support needs of Thomas.

Features

• Thomas continues to live in an environment that is most familiar to him.

- There will be a small micro board (see page 98). This micro board consists of three people (a family member/advocate, a co-trustee, and a Personal Network member). This micro board will have the authority to contract with CLBC. This funding will allow the micro board to contract with service providers. They will also monitor the quality of the care.
- Two or more compatible people will live in the home with Thomas and provide a caring and harmonious living environment. In return, they will live rent free and enjoy the home as is customary under traditional rental contracts.
- Should it become necessary to sell the home, the will contains a provision that the trustees can do so and use the funds from this transaction to acquire an equivalent home for Thomas's benefit. Any surplus funds will be placed in the family trust.
- As the trust owns the property, it will most likely not qualify for the homeowner's grant or supplement.

EXAMPLE FOUR

Surinder, living in a condominium near the family home

Background

Gopal and Dal purchased a two-bedroom condominium for their 28-year-old son, Surinder. The complex is located within three blocks of the family home.

Financing

Total cost of condominium: $170,000.
Down payment from the parents: $140,000.
Surinder's monthly mortgage payments are approximately $300 over a twenty year period.

Features

- Ownership of the home is between the parents and Surinder. As financial protection, Surrinder granted his parents enduring power of attorney.
- Upon the parents' death, complete ownership of the home goes to Surinder. Surinder's sister and her husband will have power of attorney.
- One of the bedrooms will be rented to a roommate for Surinder.
- A team comprised of a representative of the family, the service delivery organization, and the family of Surinder's roommate will oversee the maintenance and operation of the condominium.

The Making of a Sanctuary

For one glorious summer in the 70's, an old tamarisk tree with wide branches sweeping down to the sand of a Greek beach was my home. Its branches opened like welcoming arms to form my front door. When friends came to call they knew I was home if they saw my sandals carefully set to one side. Inside there was a special crook in one branch that held my cup and toothbrush and plenty of twigs to drape my scarves on. My tree gentled the sun's rays by day and let the stars peek through at night. I felt safe and sheltered by this kind tree. My tree space felt lived in, by me, by others before me and of course by various wildlife who shared it with me. It was definitely the place that felt the most like home during that sun-kissed summer.

One of our treasured family stories is the account of my mother, who upon reading a letter containing my starry eyed account of my life in Greece, burst into tears and wailed, "She's living in a tree. A tree!" For her, my breezy home was not and never would be a home.

That's the thing about a home. It is a very personal feeling. Not so much a place as a space. It is a space that breathes and nourishes us. A space becomes a home when it opens to us as we are, and when we, in turn, get worn into it. Creating this kind of home space when a person is vulnerable or isolated is complex. As families we are often caught in the paradoxical challenge of finding spaces that both open doors and secure locks. This is why cultivating and consulting caring connections beyond us is so important for our relatives. Standing together, we can peek out, open the curtains of our own comfort zones and imagine the living, breathing spaces our loved ones can grow their way into. And out of. Just as no tree lives for forever, no home, no matter how well planned, financed and built, is ever permanent. True durability lies in the long arms of others who will care for our relatives beyond our lifetime. It is an embrace that will nourish and honour the spirit of our loved ones wherever they may live. ∎

Vickie Cammack

Worksheet 6

Welcome mat

These are questions you can discuss with your relative. Have some fun and use a variety of props to facilitate your discussion: perhaps have your relative draw a few pictures or make a collage of cutouts from magazines.

What kind of home would you like to live in?_____

_____

Would you like to live by yourself or with other people?_____

_____

Who would you like to help you live in your own home?_____

_____

What would this person help you with?_____

_____

Where do you want to live?_____

_____

Why do you want to live there?_____

_____

What do you want to live close to? (a park, church, recreation centre, bus route, shops, and so on.) _____

_____

What is your favourite room?_____

_____

Do you have a favourite chair? Would you like to have one? Which room would you place it in?

_____

Where would you place your favourite things?_____

_____

What kind of furniture will you need for your own place?_____

_____

What furniture from your family home would you like to have in your own home?_____

_____

Would you keep a pet? What kind?_____

_____

Would you like a garden?_____

_____

Do you like to cook? If so, would you like to have a big kitchen?_____

_____

Would you like to have a quiet room?_____

_____

Which room would you like to have music in?_____

_____

Do you like doing dishes?_____

_____

Do you like to clean the house?_____

_____

Do you like to mow the lawn?_____

_____

How would you decorate:

Your living room? _____

_____

Your bedroom? _____

_____

Your entrance? _____

_____

What colour would you paint the outside of your house?_____

_____

How would you welcome visitors to your home?_____

_____

When you came home at the end of the day, what would be the first thing you would do?

_____

Worksheet 7

When is a house a home?

Here are some simple guidelines and questions to help you evaluate the home-like quality of residential services.

Whose house is it?

Are the individuals who live in the house the ones to determine its structure and tone or is the house geared to suit the staff hired to provide service?

Use your home and your own life as yardsticks for comparison. Do not accept, "well, it's better than where they were." Instead, ask yourself, "Is it as good as I have now?" and "Is it as good as I would want for myself?"

Look around

Are there locks where they are not needed; that is, on the refrigerator, on the clothes closets, and so on?

Are there no locks where they are needed; that is, on bathroom doors, bedroom doors, filing cabinets, medicine cabinets, and so on?

Do people have the same amount and variety of possessions and personal articles as other people their age?

What does it feel like?

Are the rooms comfortable? How about the couch? The chairs? Could you relax here? Does the place feel like a home?

Take a moment to listen

Can you go somewhere for a little peace and quiet? Are there conversations among the people who live here?

Smell

Do you get a scent of home made dinner on the stove or dessert in the oven, or do you smell institutional cleaners and odors?

Taste

Would you enjoy the food that is served or would you merely tolerate it?

Ask

What are the rules? Are they excessive or overly restrictive? Do they make sense to you? Who makes the rules?

Infer

Do the people who live here experience a home with some added support, programming, and needed supervision? Or do they experience an institutional program with a few home-like qualities?

Analyze

What compromises have been made in the name of budget limitations, programming practices, staff needs, and so on? In what ways do these compromises detract from a home-like atmosphere?

Ask yourself

If an opening came up tomorrow, would I ask to move in?

making
sound
decisions

> Compassion is maturity
> and maturity is acceptance.
> Maturity is precisely
> the acceptance of yourself
> with your own flaws,
> as well as others
> with their flaws.
>
> JEAN VANIER

More than we bargained for

"THERE WAS A PERIOD when Rick didn't live with us. At the time we thought we were doing the right thing. He was getting pretty big and pretty bored and we thought he'd be better off with people his own age. My wife and I were both working, and we thought it would be best for all of us."

George's voice softens as he discusses what he calls Rick's little adventure. Rick moved to a farm community where he lived in a group home with eight other young people his own age.

"At first it went okay for Rick, that is, but not for us. We were in shock for weeks. Next to burying my wife, driving away from that home was the hardest thing I ever had to do. Anyway, new people, and new things to do everyday kept Rick happy for a while."

Rick is quite transparent. It is easy to tell if he's happy or not. He wouldn't tell George and his wife what was bothering him but after a while he looked so glum they knew something was wrong. It took them some time to get to the bottom of it.

One night George had popped over to the house to drop off some strawberries he had just picked at the U-Pick down the road. Staff was watching television and the residents were all in their rooms. It turned out that this was common practice. In fact, it was the nightly routine. The evening shift was sending everyone to their own room at 8:30 every evening. No one was allowed to watch TV, use a radio or CD player, or make any noise.

"It was just like the bloody Air Force, back in World War Two," George explains. "No, it was worse. Lights out over there was at 10:00 p.m. for the crews who had to be up early for a flying mission. As long as we observed the blackout we could do what we pretty well wanted to."

Rick's life was completely regulated at the home, George explained.

"Their lives were controlled from top to bottom. Heck, in the six months he was there, he had four supervisors. It was a regular revolving door. Even the little things were controlled. One supervisor lasted five days. His big thing was to serve all the food from pots on the stove. After he was gone the next supervisor changed the routine. All food was to be placed in serving dishes on the table! That's the way it worked for everything. No privacy, no respect, and no choice."

It was too much for Rick and his parents. George and his wife invited Rick to move back home.

"We thought we were giving Rick more choices when he moved into the group home. Instead, we got more than we bargained for."

One of the things that bothered Rick about his group home experience was the withdrawal of his spending privileges. Any of his own money, including the comforts allowance he received from government, had to be placed in a bank account that could be accessed by staff. And they often did, buying things he didn't ask for or want.

continued on page 84

Making sound decisions

When you get right down to it, worrying about the safety and security of our relatives is a paradox. On the one hand, we want to protect them from discrimination, exploitation, abuse, neglect, and injury. On the other hand, we want them to have a good life: a life where they enjoy themselves; where they get to try new things; a life where their choices are respected. We want to teach our loved ones how to survive and work through adversity. We want them to learn from their mistakes, as all of us must. We want people to recognize their ability to make decisions and to support them to make sound decisions. This type of self-determination makes a life worth living.

It's a delicate balancing act faced by families the world over: keeping our relatives safe while at the same time respecting their choices.

Make no mistake about it. This balancing act is a tough challenge. Families find it difficult. So do service providers. So does government and its institutions. Fortunately, British Columbia has developed a legal option which enables our adult family members to get the support they need in order to make good and safe decisions without taking away their decision-making power thereby depriving them of their rights as citizens.

This Step will describe Representation Agreements, an alternative to adult guardianship. For those with young children, this discussion about Representation Agreements won't be relevant until your relative turns 19. For information on choosing a guardian for your minor children, see Choosing a guardian for children under the age of 19 on page 96.

It starts with choice

A good life includes honouring the choices of our relative. This means recognizing their tastes, preferences, and values; it also

> Do not see me as your client. I am your fellow citizen. See me as your neighbour. Help me learn what I want to know.
> NORMAN KUNC

george's story

continued from page 82

"After my wife died I decided I would use my money to keep Rick out of group living arrangements like that. Since he was in good health he was able to purchase a life insurance policy outright. This would nearly double the size of Rick's trust. George was quite worried that Rick would be taken advantage of by some unscrupulous person. "Rick isn't a whiz with money but he is careful with small amounts," George explained. He wanted Rick to have easy access to his money, but he wanted some checks on his spending. So he set up a trust. Not a discretionary trust but an income trust.

"I've got the local credit union acting as my trustee now. They're good at managing and investing the money. But just to make sure they keep Rick's interests in mind, I've appointed a co-trustee from Rick's Personal Network. And to top it all off, my Will instructs the trustees to seek advice from PLAN. All this may sound complicated, but it acts like a system of checks and balances.

"When all is said and done, I'm finally getting what I bargained for. Rick's choices are respected and so are mine. You can't beat that." ■

means acknowledging our relative's ability to discriminate, to select, and to choose. We know how determined our relatives can be to express their approval or disapproval. We know they often are aware of their limitations and exercise prudent judgment in the face of it. We know they have views and opinions on a variety of topics. Unfortunately, not everyone is aware, understands or accepts the capability of our family member.

The assumption of others that our family members don't have opinions or cannot make decisions is an additional handicap. This can lead to ignoring their wishes and eventually making all decisions, big and small, on their behalf.

Choice is like a muscle: if not exercised, it will atrophy.

We want the people involved with our relative to see what we see: a person capable of making their intentions known. We want the people in their lives to be patient, to be willing to listen, and to watch, and if necessary to be willing to learn our relative's unique and perhaps non-verbal communication style. We know all behaviour is a form of communication and we want our relatives surrounded by people who will take the time to search for that meaning.

We are wary of people who won't make an effort to learn how our relatives express themselves, who are too busy, or who ignore—and perhaps worse—think they know what is best for our relative.

However, once there is recognition of their choice making ability, we can turn our attention to supporting our relative to make decisions. This may mean in certain circumstances, speaking or making decisions on their behalf. We do this informally when we set up a joint bank account or when we accompany them to a medical appointment. This type of supported decision-making is formally recognized in British Columbia when our relative creates a Representation Agreement.

We believe in nurturing the decision-making ability of our relative rather than giving someone else the power to make decisions on their behalf. The decision-making ability of our relative can be nurtured by:

- respecting their inherent decision-making ability
- enabling their own, authentic decision-making voice
- presenting them with genuine choices

- helping them to sort out and understand the options, and
- supporting them in making the actual decision.

In realty, many people with disabilities are offered few choices in their lives. Instead, they are treated as an object to whom things are done. They become passive and submissive. When we surround them with people who respect their capacity to make decisions, we also create the conditions for our relative to become a self-advocate. This reduces the risk of exploitation, neglect, and abuse. Ultimately our relatives are safer when they are able to speak for themselves.

Take Tim's situation, for example. When we first met Tim his care-givers made all his decisions. They decided what he should wear, what he should do during the day, what time he should have dinner, and so on. These decisions were based on what suited his caregiver's sched-ule. Tim was never consulted. For example, Tim loved country music but his caregivers didn't so he never had the opportunity to listen to the country music station.

Over time, Tim retreated so far into the background of his own life that he might as well have been invisible.

Fortunately Tim and his family joined PLAN. As his Personal Network developed, so did the relationship between Tim and his staff. Eventually new caregivers were hired based on their willingness to learn Tim's communication style.

Change is a constant. It is hard to predict what we or our loved ones will have to adjust to, what critical decisions will have to be made in the future. We can make educated guesses about some of the areas we want protected for our relative but there are no guarantees. Rather than wasting our energy on trying to control the uncontrollable, we suggest you prepare for any eventuality by providing your relative with the best possible people to assist them in making their own decisions.

Honouring capability: assuming, respecting, and supporting choice.

Relationships are the foundation of sound decision-making

By now it should come as no surprise that relationships and Personal Networks have additional benefits—they enable good decision-making and assist to protect and keep your relative safe.

The first order of business, therefore, is to consolidate your relative's friends and supporters into a network. Members of a network can monitor the services and programs your relative receives; they can also advocate to ensure the quality of those services and programs.

Network members are often more than willing to support good financial, health, and personal care decision-making for your relative. Some network members are willing to be appointed as Representatives in the Representation Agreement your relative creates. In some cases, the creation of a Representation Agreement can be the spark for establishing a Personal Network for your relative.

Representation Agreements: supported decision-making

Standard (sometimes referred to as Section 7) Representation Agreements enable adults to get decision-making support without having to go to court or without having to be declared incapable. This is an exciting, practical, and low cost option for your relative.

It is important to recognize that a Representation Agreement belongs to your relative and not to you. You can help your relative create one, but it is a legal plan signed by your relative conferring authority to Representatives they choose to assist them to manage their own affairs. If you want a Representation Agreement yourself— and that would be advisable—you should create your own!

The *Representation Agreement Act* assumes your relative has the legal capacity to sign the agreement, make a mark or indicate in some other way who they want to assist them to make decisions. There is no up front test of capacity to create a Representation Agreement. However, there is always the possibility their capability could be challenged by a bank, hospital or someone who is not familiar with people with disabilities making their own decisions. This is why the Representation Agreement makes provision to describe the way your relative communicates, the nature of their limitations, and the relationship the Representatives have with your relative. It is prudent to be transparent and thorough when you assist your relative in creating a Representation Agreement.

Two important factors in determining capability—should it ever be challenged—include:

- the existence of a trusting relationship between the adult and their Representative(s); and
- evidence the adult is able to express choices, preferences, and feelings of approval and disapproval of others.

All forms of communication—verbal and non-verbal—are recognized in preparing and signing Representation Agreements.

There are actually two types of Representation Agreements, Standard and Enhanced. The Standard Agreement covers routine financial, health, and personal care decisions and is more than adequate to provide support for most of the decisions our relative will make. These decisions are spelled out in detail in the regulations to the *Representation Agreement Act*. See the box on page 91 for details on Enhanced Representation Agreements.

Standard Representation Agreements cover:

- routine management of financial affairs: banking, applying for and dealing with benefits, insuring or selling motor vehicles, managing existing loans and insurance, dealing with income tax, making or disposing of investments, and so on
- minor health care: medical examinations, immunizations, medications
- major health care: surgery, general anesthetic, kidney dialysis, chemotherapy
- personal care: diet, exercise, living arrangements, maintaining spiritual and religious traditions, arranging home support, caring for pets.

The Standard Representation Agreement does not require a lawyer, although you can retain one if you wish. Otherwise, the Agreement can be prepared by your relative in conjunction with you and other supporters. The Nidus Personal Planning Resource Centre provides a self-help kit and will assist you through the process of developing a Representation Agreement for your relative (see box below). PLAN also assists in developing Representation Agreements.

The Benefits of Representation Agreements

An attractive feature of a Representation Agreement is its adaptability. It can be tailored to suit the exact circumstances of your relative.

Representation Agreements have been developed for most PLAN members, regardless of the nature and extent of their disability and vulnerability and regardless of how they communicate.

Representation Agreements:

- strengthen the voice of our relatives and ensure that their views, values, and beliefs are front and centre

Nidus Personal Planning Resource Centre and Registry

The Nidus Personal Planning Resource Centre and Registry is a non-profit, charitable organization that provides information and assistance with Representation Agreements and other personal planning tools.

Nidus offers a Self-help Kit for Representation Agreements for Supported Decision-making. Nidus also operates a centralized Registry for personal planning documents.

Visit the Nidus website for more information at www.nidus.ca or contact them by telephone at: 604-408-7414 or by email at info@nidus.ca.

> We have got to
> put our human
> spirit on the line
> if we hope to
> communicate with
> others at all.
> Maybe that is
> when people feel
> cared for,
> when they feel
> that sense
> of human spirit.
>
> MARGARET SOMMERVILLE

- provide a test of capability that reflects the abilities of our relatives. The traditional test of capability to sign personal planning documents like Enduring Powers of Attorney is too high and overly reliant on intellectual ability. Many of our relatives can't meet this test because of a developmental disability, a brain injury, dementia or a stroke. This emphasis on intellectual ability ignores other recognized ways of "knowing" including social capability; that is, your ability to relate to others and convey trust. Representation Agreements acknowledge these factors. In addition to the traditional intellectual factors, Representation Agreements also include trusting relationships as an important consideration in determining capability.
- accept all forms of communication—verbal and non-verbal— whether it is a nod, a blink of an eye or use of a communication device
- give status to friends, family members, and members of Personal Networks. Many of us don't realize that when our sons and daughters turn 19 we are no longer their legal guardian. Representation Agreements give status to family, particularly parents
- create an opportunity for serious discussion about basic safety and security concerns for our relatives
- create a vehicle for formalizing existing relationships and forming a network of support
- create the means for a working partnership among caregivers, professionals, government workers, friends, family members, and our relative
- lastly, Representation Agreements provide parents with peace of mind.

Basic facts about Representation Agreements:

- anyone over the age of 19 years can make a standard Agreement even if they cannot currently manage their affairs or sign a traditional contract
- Representation Agreements authorize people to assist your relative manage their affairs without your relative losing their own decision-making rights
- everyone is assumed to be capable of signing a standard Representation Agreement
- all forms of communication are accepted, verbal and non-verbal
- to prevent abuse and exploitation of an adult who creates a Representation Agreement, a number of safeguards are available:
  - all agreements must be witnessed
  - a Monitor must be appointed for routine financial decisions
  - the actions of Representatives may be challenged, and
  - the Office of Public Guardian and Trustee has the authority to investigate complaints.

Section 9: Enhanced Representation Agreements

Section 9—or Enhanced Representation Agreements—covers all health, financial, and personal care decisions no matter how complex. This includes end of life decisions. Enhanced Agreements must be drafted by a lawyer.

Some of you may be more familiar with enduring Powers of Attorney which are more limited than Enhanced Representation Agreements. Enduring Powers of Attorney cover financial and legal matters but not health care and, therefore, not end of life decisions. Most lawyers will suggest that their clients use an enduring Power of Attorney for legal and financial matters and a Representation Agreement for health and personal care matters.

The test of capacity for signing an Enhanced Representation Agreement or an Enduring Power of Attorney is higher than for the Standard Representation Agreement.

Should I consider Legal Guardianship?

Traditional legal guardianship permits another person to take over the affairs and decision-making for an adult who has been declared incapable by the courts. That guardian is called a Committee (pronounced Kaw–Mit–TEE with emphasis on the last syllable). A legally appointed Committee has complete power to make financial, medical, and legal decisions for the person. There are two types of Committee:

- committee of the estate: authority to make financial and legal decisions, and
- committee of the person: authority to make health and personal care decisions.

Representation Agreements were developed as an alternative to this type of guardianship. We have reservations about Committeeship:

1. Most guardianship orders are blunt instruments. Even though adults may only need help in certain areas of decision-making, the guardianship orders are not easily tailored. All of a person's financial and personal decision-making power may be removed. The adult can no longer assist with the decision-making process. In the eyes of the law, they are no longer a capable person.

2. Obtaining a guardianship order is costly, intrusive, and time-consuming.

3. Guardianship doesn't allow for joint or supported decision-making. It's an all or nothing proposition.

4. People with intellectual impairments and other noticeable differences are usually presumed to be incapable which makes it even tougher to assert their capability.

5. The appointment of a Committee involves the Office of the Public Guardian and Trustee (OPGT). The OPGT typically reviews the adult's financial records annually. This potentially adds another layer of complication and paperwork.

Few people with disabilities will ever need this form of guardianship. In the past, some parents applied to the courts to become Committee of their adult son or daughter assuming this would give them enhanced status when dealing with government or service providers. Unfortunately, this proved frustrating and costly without providing any more influence or authority.

Representation Agreements are an economical alternative to protect a vulnerable person without declaring them incapable. It also gives status to caring, trusted friends and family members. Traditional legal guardianship and Committeeship should only be considered as a last resort.

Summary of Legal Options

- The Standard Representation Agreement (Section 7): covers routine legal, financial, health, and personal care decisions
- The Enhanced Representation Agreement (Section 9): covers all legal, financial, health, and personal care decisions
- Enduring Powers of Attorney: covers legal and financial matters but not health and personal care decisions

- Temporary Substitute Decision-Maker: used to seek permission for health care when a Representation Agreement or Committeeship does not exist.
- Committee of the estate and of the person: authority to make financial, legal, health, and personal care decisions on behalf of another person.

Types of decision-making

There are three broad areas of decision-making that affect your relative's life:

1. Health/Medical Decisions
2. Financial Decisions
3. Personal Care Decisions

Personal Networks and Representation Agreements are critical to each. Combined with a number of non-legal options, they offer further assurance that decisions will be made that protect and enhance the quality of life of your relative.

1. HEALTH/MEDICAL DECISION-MAKING You can divide this into emergency and non-emergency decision-making.

Families want assurance their relative will receive medical treatment in the event of an emergency, especially if the doctors are unable to obtain legal consent. You need not worry. Doctors and hospitals in British Columbia can and do provide emergency medical treatment when it is needed regardless of whether consent can be obtained.

For non-emergency health care, the experience is more varied. Many adults with disabilities enjoy a long-standing relationship with their family doctor. They know each other's abilities and communication styles. In these situations, the capacity of the person with the disability to give consent is simply not an issue. The physician is willing to take the time to give the individual the opportunity to express their wishes.

In other situations, it has become common practice for the doctor or health care provider to consult with parents or other close relatives around health care treatment for the adult with a disability. The medical profession has long recognized relationships of trust and caring.

In these situations, supported decision-making is already working. It is best to formalize these relationships by having your relative create a Representation Agreement.

If you do not have a Representation Agreement or Committee-ship and you are found to be incapable, then your doctor, health care provider or hospital must find someone to give consent for health care.

> We become what we behold. We shape our tools and then tools shape us.
> MARSHALL MCLUHAN

There is provision in statute to appoint a Temporary Substitute Decision Maker (TSDM). The health care provider chooses from the TSDM list in the following order:

- spouse, including common law and same-sex partner
- adult child
- parent
- brother or sister
- another relative by birth or adoption.

The TSDM must be over 19, capable, and know the person. The TSDM must have been in contact with them in the past 12 months and must not have had a dispute with them. This list is focused on family.

If no family member qualifies, the Public Guardian and Trustee has the power to choose someone and can authorize a friend.

If there is no family involvement or you would prefer someone you trust to help with health care decisions, then it is best to make a Representation Agreement.

2. FINANCIAL DECISIONS There are a number of legal and non-legal options to protect the financial assets of your relative, prevent exploitation, negligence or impulsive purchases, and to ensure good financial decision-making.

The first, of course, is a Standard Representation Agreement. Have a look again at the list of routine financial decision-making options. In some cases, an Enhanced or Section 9 Agreement may be useful. So might an Enduring Power of Attorney.

An enduring power of attorney is a written document that allows a person to confer authority to someone else to make financial decisions on their behalf. When you confer this authority on someone else you don't lose your own authority. The power of attorney can be revoked at any time by the person who conferred it.

Both Enhanced Representation Agreements and Enduring Powers of Attorney have a higher, more traditional legal test of capability which your adult relative may not pass.

Trusts are another option used by families to protect the financial assets of their relative and to ensure the funds are used in their best

Now that we can do anything, what will we do?

BRUCE MAU

Choosing a guardian for children under the age of 19

It is difficult to discuss who should take care of our children under the age of 19 should we die unexpectedly.

Unfortunately it does happen leaving the surviving children, remaining relatives, and friends in legal limbo. The courts become involved and a judge makes a custody order. You cannot assume grandparents, godparents or other choices you think are obvious will automatically be given responsibility. More than 40 per cent of Canadian parents have not legally appointed a guardian for their children. (NOTE: Contrary to popular belief, you cannot appoint a guardian for your adult children in your Will. See Step 5 for more details.)

You must add a guardianship clause to your Will. One of the toughest decisions faced by parents is determining who to appoint as legal guardian of our minor children. To ease this emotionally difficult process and to prevent further upset, here are some suggestions to assist you in choosing a guardian:

- list your parental values, your aspirations for your children, as well as any religious, financial or cultural concerns;
- choose the person who comes closest to your parenting style and who would guide your children the way you intend to guide them. A child's aunt or uncle is a common trusted choice, followed by close family friends. Trust in that person's judgment is paramount;
- try to select someone close to your age rather than someone of your parent's generation. Your parents may be excellent grandparents but they may not be able to manage another set of children, especially through the teenage years;
- becoming a guardian adds additional financial as well as emotional responsibilities. In recognition of this, some parents take out a life insurance policy naming the guardian as beneficiary;
- parents of other children with disabilities are a good source of advice. Because of their common bond, parents often choose each other as guardians.

interest. Step Five explores this option in more detail (see page 109). Trustees can be appointed at any time to manage trust funds.

In the past, many families considered becoming Committee of the Estate in order to protect, manage, and invest the financial assets of their adult relative with a disability. This procedure has a number of disadvantages:

- obtaining Committee involves the courts and is time-consuming and expensive
- reporting on the management and expenditure of money is tedious and costly
- guidelines to protect and invest the assets may be too conservative for productive money management.

Other practical approaches used by families to safeguard their family member's assets include:

- establishing a joint bank account with your son or daughter
- purchasing property in joint title (see Patricia's story on page 71).

3. PERSONAL CARE DECISIONS This is an area of decision-making that is by far the most elusive because the forces are largely out of our control. Our relatives will likely be dealing with paid caregivers or service providers and educators for the rest of their lives. They will make daily decisions which will have a huge impact on our relative.

We can't predict the future of government funding for these critical supports and the repercussions on the quality of programs and services. We are pleased that regulations and policy set standards for service providers. And we acknowledge the value of accreditation and formal evaluation. But we know this doesn't go far enough. These tend to focus on broad system standards. They don't address the personal daily circumstances of each of our relatives.

Monitoring and advocacy are natural extensions of our parenting skills. While we are alive we can engage with service providers. We know how important it is to maintain a relationship with them. We have a good idea of how much work this requires and how much time it takes. If there is a concern we can do something about it. We can join

Paid service should supplement —not supplant— good, old-fashioned human contact, warmth and love.

an agency's Boards of Directors. We can create our own society! As in other areas of decision-making, Personal Networks and Representation Agreements are essential. Here are additional options and resources for you to consider.

Individualized Funding

Most service providers receive their funding under contract from government. Often one agency or organization provides the full range of services needed by the individual. That is, they own or lease the homes, provide the staff, and offer residential, employment, recreational, and other support services. People who use these services often have very little say over what happens to them. Many parents and individuals are now promoting a new approach called individualized funding. So are governments. For example, the British Government recently created legislation making it mandatory to offer Direct Funding to all individuals with disabilities in England and Wales should they request it.

Community Living BC also offers individualized funding on a limited basis. See Resources, page 187.

Individualized funding gives money directly to the individual with a disability or their Representatives to enable them to purchase the goods and services they require. Individualized funding covers the cost of food, clothing, shelter, transportation, and technical aids as well as program and personal care supports. The individual—with the help of their supporters—can then determine where to live, with whom to live, who to hire, and so on.

Microboards

Imagine a non-profit society that exists only to provide programs and services to your relative. That's what a micro board is.

A microboard is a small (hence the name, micro) society with a board of directors. The board of directors, usually no more than five, is comprised of committed family members and friends. This board of directors receives funding from government on behalf of the person with a disability and negotiates with service providers to provide the support services. The board of directors, along with the person with a disability, directs and customizes these support services. Microboards are a successful variation on individualized funding and personalized services.

Microboards serve a variety of other purposes as well because they create opportunities for relationships of support to flourish. Overall, they allow people to achieve greater control over their personal support needs. The Vela Microboard Society pioneered microboards in British Columbia and around the world. It is an excellent resource. For more information see Resources, page 187.

Choice in Supports for Independent Living (CSIL)

Another example of personalized funding is the Choice in Supports for Independent Living Services (CSIL). CSIL is a form of individualized funding available through the Ministry of Health Services to "give British Columbians with daily personal care needs more flexibility in managing their home support services." CSIL is a self-managed model of care. Individuals receive funds directly to purchase their home support services. They assume full responsibility for the management, coordination, and financial accountability of their services. Participants recruit, hire, train, supervise, and schedule their own staff. Anyone needing help with those responsibilities can arrange for a Client Support Group (five people chosen by the participant who register as a non-profit society) to manage the support services on their behalf.

Advocacy

Yeats, the Irish poet observed: "things fall apart; the centre cannot hold." Human services are human creations and are, therefore—by definition—imperfect. Things can fall apart.

Families know this instinctively. Our work at PLAN bears this out. We are often called to support an individual, family or Personal Network as they advocate for change and improvement in a program or service. People who know our relative make the best advocates. They may not know all the details of service provision and funding but they are

As I get older,
I get smaller.
I see other parts
of the world
I didn't see before.
Other points
of view.
I see outside
myself more.

NEIL YOUNG

grounded in what is best for our relative and will fight on their behalf. There are many groups in British Columbia who offer advocacy and support. See Resources on page 187.

See Resources on page 187.

An effective personal advocate and monitor is someone who:

- cares about our relatives
- knows their requirements
- has good problem solving and negotiating skills
- is free of conflict of interest
- is self-confident and willing to be assertive if necessary
- is willing to seek out—and follow—good advice.

We have discovered that Personal Networks are a great training ground for advocates. Parents can impart their skill and wisdom and teach by doing.

Lastly, we should point out the value of teaching our relative self-advocacy skills. They will learn about their rights and responsibilities; how to speak up for themselves; how to support other self-advocates; and gain confidence. There are excellent written resources and many organizational supports in British Columbia. For more information, see Resources, page 187.

For more information, see Resources, page 187.

Good decision-making for our relative means:

- they actively participate
- their views are sought and taken into consideration
- they are surrounded by caring, knowledgeable, trustworthy people who can assist with their decision-making, and communicate their decisions
- their needs are the primary consideration, not those of staff or the service system
- the focus is on their abilities
- their tastes, preferences, motives, and ability to discriminate are taken seriously
- their risks, failures, and mistakes are learning opportunities
- all their methods of communication, both verbal and non-verbal, are recognized as valid.

Progress always starts with bold ideas .

JANE JACOBS

Choices

We suggest that you support your relative to make good decisions by asking yourself the following questions:

- What choices do they have now?
- What experience do they have with decision-making?
- What decisions can they make independently?
- What decisions will they need help with?
- What informal arrangements can be made to assist with decision-making?
- Would they benefit from a Representation Agreement?

Conclusion: the secret to good decision-making

There is no magic to the task of keeping our relatives safe while at the same time respecting their choices. A tilt in the direction of over protection could lead, at the extreme, to a barren existence. A tilt in the direction of complete autonomy could lead to abuse and exploitation. The secret is balance. And checks.

And the best way to do that is by assembling the best people and resources. A Personal Network—combined with a Representation Agreement, control over the funding, and ongoing advocacy—is the best safety net we know. ∎

If you look long enough, eventually you will be able to see me.

MARGARET ATWOOD

Diving

WHEN I WROTE THIS fictional meditation, I had not yet read Jean-Dominique Bauby's extraordinary book *The Diving-Bell and the Butterfly* (see Resources, page 187). His story is better known now as a result of the movie of the same name. At the age of 45, French journalist Bauby suffered a massive stroke that left him without speech and movement. He was, as he says, "like a mind in a jar." Patiently, letter by letter, Bauby tells his story, using one eyelid to signal at what point in the chorus line of letters his friend is to stop transcribing. Bauby's reality is bright, vivid, and compelling.

What would you do in a similiar situation?

You are heading to the grocery store on a sunny Saturday morning. You are a careful driver but your mind is elsewhere—on automatic pilot. Suddenly an approaching car jumps lanes and heads towards you. In a terrifying instant your life changes. After the impact you lose consciousness.

You wake up in the hospital. The pain is excruciating. You are unable to move your arms and legs. Then you discover you can't speak. A doctor and a nurse are hovering over you. They are asking a lot of questions. They want to know your blood type. You aren't able to respond. For one thing, you are in shock. For another, they aren't watching your facial gestures and you have no other way of communicating.

They are now explaining what needs to happen to you. No one seems to notice the fear in your eyes. You hear medical terms you don't understand. You're scared and all alone. Where is your wife? Have they tried to reach her?

Suddenly you are placed on a stretcher and rushed down the hallway into an elevator, then down another hallway and into an operating room. Your last thoughts before the anesthetic takes hold are of …

Who would you think of? Your spouse, your children, your parents, your brothers and sisters, your friends? Or your lawyer, your mechanic, your dentist?

You do survive. The hospital is crowded but they manage to find a semi-private room for you. And they locate your spouse. She comes in several hours after you return from surgery. She immediately understands your terror. You are covered with blood. The needle from the IV tube is already causing noticeable swelling and bruising. Your wife calls a nurse. They respond immediately. They are cooperative and friendly. They didn't expect you to wake up so soon. They were busy elsewhere. The IV tube is adjusted and they give you a warm sponge bath. Eventually you drift off to sleep, comforted by the presence of your wife. At least you are not alone.

When your wife and friends are around, you feel safer and your needs are met. They notice when you are uncomfortable. They do all the little things that make your stay tolerable.

On one occasion you had to contend with an inexperienced intern who insisted on giving you a needle in your arm even though he couldn't find a sizable vein. You were helpless to protest. Your arm became a personal challenge to him. When a colleague from work arrived, it was bruised and bloodied. Within minutes he had your wife on the phone. She spoke to the charge nurse and a notation was made on your chart. It won't happen again, they promised. It doesn't.

What keeps you safe during your hospital stay? Is it hospital rules and regulations? Is it the professional training of medical staff? Is it the nurses and doctors? Or is it friends and family?

Friends and family remove the cloak of anonymity. With them you become a person again. It's not that professional paid care isn't important; it's just that you are more than the sum of your health needs. Make no mistake about it, this move from being an object of service to a real person depends on your relationships.

Why would it be any different for people with disabilities?

It isn't. However, we often make the error of assuming professional paid care is all that is necessary to keep people with disabilities safe and guarantee choice. Programs, professional supports, rules, and regulations have their limitations. Paid service should supplement—not supplant—good, old-fashioned human contact, warmth and love. ■

Al Etmanski

Worksheet 8

Preparing for a representation agreement

Use this worksheet to organize your supported decision-making choices.
After completing this worksheet you will be able to assist your relative in drafting their
Representation Agreement. We suggest you contact PLAN or the Nidus Resource Centre
for further assistance in drafting and activating a standard Representation Agreement.

This worksheet does not give any legal advice. A Representation Agreement is a legal
contract which must be drafted in accordance with the *Representation Agreement Act*.
The Representatives and Monitors appointed under the agreement are accepting
responsibility and liability from the adult, so it is important that they understand their
duties and responsibilities.

A. Checklist

MEDICAL DECISION-MAKING

YES   NO   I have discussed issues of medical consent with my relative's doctor.

YES   NO   The doctor accepts consent from my relative for medical treatment.

YES   NO   The doctor accepts my consent for medical care on my relative's behalf.

FINANCIAL DECISION-MAKING

YES   NO   I have set up an income trust.

YES   NO   I have set up a discretionary trust.

YES   NO   My relative has a RDSP.

YES   NO   My relative has a bank account.

YES   NO   Withdrawals from that bank account are protected by:

- joint signature for withdrawals

- my family member is well known to bank employees

- funds in the account are kept to a minimum

- don't need to be protected.

PERSONAL CARE DECISION-MAKING

YES   NO   My family member has an advocate(s).

YES   NO   The services my relative receives are monitored by a separate and independent agency.

YES   NO   Housing supports are kept separate from other services.

YES   NO   Staff understand and support the importance of family involvement.

YES   NO   Staff understand and welcome the involvement of spouses, friends, and members of the Personal Network.

YES   NO   Service and program staff recognize the importance of offering and respecting my family member's choices.

YES   NO   Family and friends provide support by reviewing services and programs on a regular basis. (NOTE: This is different from the service plans developed by service providers.)

YES   NO   Members of the Personal Network are familiar with the personal care issues.

B. Information

GENERAL

Who does my relative trust? _____

Who would I trust to assist my relative with decision-making?_____

Who understands my relative's communication style? _____

MEDICAL DECISIONS

Who is my relative's doctor? _____

What assistance would they need to make medical decisions? _____

_____

Who would my relative accept to assist with medical decision-making?_____

_____

What aspect of their medical care do I think my relative might understand?_____

_____

What formal arrangements do I need to make to ensure medical care is easily available to my

relative? _____

_____

FINANCIAL DECISIONS

My relative's trustees are: _____

_____

My financial advisors are: _____

_____

My relative has the following bank accounts: _____

_____

Signing authority includes: _____

Who would be willing to assist my relative in making financial decisions?_____

_____

I have asked the following individual to monitor the trust I have set up for my relative: _____

_____

PERSONAL CARE DECISIONS

My relative's advocate is: _____

The independent agency that monitors services is:_____

_____

Who would be willing to assist my relative in making lifestyle and personal care decisions?

_____

achieving
financial security
wills, trusts, and
the new RDSP

Then, when he had flown a while longer,
something brightened toward the north.
It caught his eye, they say.
And then he flew right up against it.

He pushed his mind through
and pulled his body after.

SKAAY, HAIDA POET AND STORYTELLER

What the heck, it can't hurt me… and it might even help

"A LOT OF PEOPLE my age have thought about this problem for most of their adult life. They hope their plans are adequate. Maybe they made a Will 30 years ago. Or maybe they hope that, magically, new plans will come together at the last minute. I don't think that's good enough.

"When you have a child with a disability you get lots of advice. But usually nothing ever materializes. So you get kind of negative. However, you have to remember that every once in a while something comes along and it does work.

"I knew if I was going to make progress I had to take chances. What the heck, I said, it can't hurt me…and it might even help."

George's involvement with other parents associated with PLAN encouraged him to think about where he was going and what he wanted to achieve. "I call it putting your house in order. They got me moving but you have to be willing to do it. It means getting organized—getting all your necessary papers together.

"My original Will is long gone. We made a new one just before my wife died. I changed it a year later to include some clauses I heard about from other families. Then I decided to change my trustee and to include a role for PLAN after I died. So I got another lawyer and she drafted a new Will. It's never really over, you know. If I find out about something better and I'm still around I'll make changes again. Actually, altering your Will is easy and not that expensive. Things are evolving and you are bound to get new ideas.

"My first goal was to make sure there were sufficient funds to look after Rick. I got advice on prescribed insured annuities and how to use life insurance to increase the size of my estate. There were things about life insurance I never knew. I just about doubled the size of my estate by buying a policy outright. Fortunately I'm in good health. And the money would be available for Rick right away after I died. It wouldn't be tied up in probate and it wouldn't be taxable.

"These were the sorts of things I knew nothing about. The fact that other parents were exploring the same things gave me confidence."

George also decided to change trust companies because he heard through the parent grapevine about a company that went the extra mile.

"I didn't figure I could take my previous trust officer out to lunch. Or for that matter that he would ever be interested in taking Rick out to lunch. I wanted a more personal approach and I got it."

For George getting to know other families helped get him moving. Looking back on it now he realizes how easy it really was. The time spent actually doing his planning was negligible compared to the time he had spent worrying. ∎

Achieving financial security: wills, trusts, and the new RDSP

This step will provide you with an overview of how to plan for and protect the financial well-being of your family member with a disability both now and in the future. Aside from a disability, many of our family members experience the additional handicap of being poor. While we are around, we can help them out in many ways, although we must keep BC disability assistance regulations in mind.

NOTE: BC disability assistance is the financial assistance that our relatives receive from the provincial government. You might have seen it as "disability benefits" or as "GAIN" in the past. It is provided through the BC Employment and Assistance program which also provides supplementary benefits such as medical and dental.

We worry most about what the future will hold. We want to put enough money aside to handle emergencies and unforeseen circumstances. We don't want our loved ones to just get by. Simply existing is not enough; we also want our family members to have a good life.

Most of us are not sufficiently wealthy to leave enough money in our estate to cover the costs of everything that our family members might possibly need. Until recently, there were limited options or tools we could use to deal with this challenge. If our family members relied on government

Step five highlights

This chapter highlights the key tools at your disposal to plan for the financial security of your relative. These include:

- will and estate planning
- discretionary trusts
- the new RDSP.

This information will help with your preparation but is no substitute for legal advice.

benefits, there was little we could do to supplement their income without it being clawed back by the provincial government.

Fortunately this is changing, particularly in British Columbia where the government is not only committed to assisting people with disabilities receive financial help from their families but is also committed to assisting families build up savings. Penalties and disincentives are being eliminated. For example, the money received from the new RDSP will NOT be clawed back (see detailed discussion on the new RDSP in Section Two below, and for ongoing updates please visit www.rdsp.com).

These changes signify that we are approaching a new partnership between families and government: a partnership based on shared responsibility which acknowledges the commitment that families have always made to the safety and well-being of their relatives with disabilities.

This chapter is divided into two main sections:
Section One: Wills, Discretionary Trusts, and Estate Planning
Section Two: The new Registered Disability Savings Plan (RDSP). The information contained in these two sections will:

- provide you with general information on drafting a Will and planning your estate
- highlight the importance of trusts, particularly discretionary trusts
- introduce you to the new Registered Disability Savings Plan (RDSP)
- discuss the relationship among government benefits, the RDSP, and discretionary trusts
- overall, help you plan for the financial security of your relative.

Assuming financial security for your loved one need not be complicated, particularly if you have thought through the issues raised in the preceding steps. Sure it's technical but the worksheet at the end of this step will help. Once you have completed it, there are plenty of good lawyers, accountants, financial and estate planners, and wealth management specialists to help you finalize your plans. PLAN keeps a current list of qualified professionals if you need a referral. Please visit www.plan.ca and click under "Resources" for the referral list.

This chapter won't replace the need to make some tough choices. The professionals you will choose are highly skilled but they rely on the clarity of your vision, your plans, and your details in order to make the right plan for your family.

Fortunately you are not alone. You can use PLAN as a back-up resource. Our advice has been sifted through the experiences of thousands of individuals and families we have supported over the past 20 years. We've learned from them all! Even those of us with little disposable income or limited assets can still leave something to help our relatives.

We pass on this accumulated wisdom knowing that being better prepared will:

- save you time and money
- assist you in selecting the right course for your loved one
- make it easier to complete your Will
- leave you with peace of mind.

You can't believe how relieved you'll feel when you've finally done it!

Wills, discretionary trusts, and estate planning

Do not be intimidated by legal language. All professions have their jargon. Some of the key words and phrases you'll encounter are summarized in Demystifying Definitions on page 151.

In praise of the imperfect will

You've heard the facts before. Over 50 per cent of Canadians die without a Will. Many others die with a Will that's out-of-date. You want to avoid joining their ranks. But you don't have all the answers. You still need to work out a few more details. You're just about there... maybe after reading this chapter.

Well, we're sorry to disappoint you. This chapter will not help you create the perfect Will. Neither will any other book. Or person, for that matter. So don't make the same mistake too many others have made. Don't wait for something that will never happen.

Now is the time to develop and execute the "imperfect" Will. It is one of the biggest gifts you can give to your family and to yourself. We feel so strongly about this we might call our next book, "In Praise of Imperfection."

What's so great about perfection anyway? Where did we get the grandiose illusion that we humans can either be perfect or get things perfect? The perfect meal or the perfect day? Maybe. But the perfect body, perfect looks, and the perfect job while living in the perfect house? Perfection is an illusion which adds unnecessary pressure and can make us feel guilty for never measuring up. Surely, absolute perfection is the job of divine personalities, beyond the scope of mere mortals. Few, if any of us, ever attain these standards. Yet we still manage to get on with our lives.

And that's precisely what we want you to do with your Will. Get on with it! Preparing and completing the imperfect Will is not the least you can do, it's the best you can do.

Beginning to create your will and estate plan

Surely the true definition of courage is to do the thing you are afraid to do.

GEORGIA BINNIE CLARK

Before you create your Will, you must be clear about the details. Every family situation is unique. You are going to rely on your family after you are gone, so it's a good idea to discuss things with them now. If the person you want to be your executor is intimidated by lawyers or has never invested money, now is the time to find out.

There are other valuable resource people you might consider talking to: extended family, friends, members of your relative's Personal Network, other families in similar circumstances, and so on.

In our experience, it helps families clarify their objectives by talking to others in similar circumstances. The more open and forthright your discussions are, the clearer your objectives will be. This will make for a more meaningful and more efficient relationship with your lawyer, accountant, and estate planning specialist. When seeking advice on estate planning, tax planning, or wealth management strategies, see Questions to ask an Advisor on page 131.

Eight key objectives

Most people want their will and estate plan to:

1. pay their debts, taxes, and other liabilities
2. provide a separate independent income for their spouse
3. distribute their assets according to their wishes
4. maximize the size of their estate for their children
5. protect the financial security of their relative with a disability (NOTE: The new RDSP and discretionary trusts are your basic tools for this.)
6. ensure that there is a guardian for their children under the age of 19
7. avoid delays, family strife, needless taxation, costly legal challenges, probate fees, and government involvement
8. allocate a portion of their estate to the charities and causes they are passionate about.

Tips from Jack Collins for securing the future

Jack Collins—one of PLAN's co-founders and a co-author of this book—knows much about the legal and financial elements of securing the future. After he retired, he dedicated his time to learning everything possible about the technical aspects of will and estate planning and how they can be coordinated with government benefits. Although he is a lay person, lawyers, financial and estate planners rely on his insights and advice.

His credibility among families is legendary. They like his plain speaking, no nonsense style. They trust him because he is one of them. Culled from his vault of expertise and its application to thousands of families, here are tips from the master!

- Get a basic Will as quickly as possible. I have seen what happens when a parent dies without a Will.
- Review your Will every two years and update it when something in your life changes. Additions and amendments (called codicils) are not costly.
- Life insurance is a good way to finance a discretionary trust. For a small monthly premium you can finance a policy. After you die the proceeds can be placed tax free—and without probate costs—into your family member's discretionary trust.
- Appoint executors and trustees who will outlive you—in other words, appoint someone younger than you—and appoint alternates just in case.
- The year of your death will likely be your highest income year because most investments are deemed sold on the day of your death and any remaining RRSPs or RRIFs get added to your income. Tax and estate planning—including donations to charity—will reduce the tax bite.
- Most of us want the trust capital as well as income to go entirely to our relative. To do so, your trust document must specifically exclude the "even handed rule" so the trustee(s) do not have to consider the rights of residual beneficiaries. If such permission is granted within the trust document then the trustees will be encouraged to spend down the capital as well as income. Please consult your lawyer on this technical point.
- Grandparents often look for ways to help secure the future of their grandchildren. Suggest they create a discretionary trust—or contribute to an RDSP—for their grandchild with a disability.

Basic questions about wills, trusts, estates, and the RDSP

Once you've added your own personalized objectives to the eight general objectives described above and you are comfortable—well, reasonably comfortable—with your answers, you are ready for the technical solutions. Here are some questions and answers to start you on your way.

NOTE: For a complete list of legal terms, see "Demystifying definitions that could definitely derail you" on page 151.

> Family is not an important thing, it's everything.
>
> MICHAEL J. FOX

WHAT IS A WILL? A Will is the legal document that tells people what to do with your estate. It helps makes life easier for those left behind by providing a plan for them to follow and by naming who is in charge.

WHAT IS ESTATE PLANNING? Estate planning is quite a broad term. It includes such things as:

- preparing your Will
- preparing a Representation Agreement for health and personal care, if appropriate
- preparing powers of attorney, advance medical directives and Living Wills or personal declarations about end of life decisions
- deciding upon issues such as executor and trustee appointment, and finding ways to minimize probate fees
- calculating your estate needs and determining the amount of life insurance needed to meet those needs
- looking at strategies to reduce income taxes at death
- advising about a trust for you or a trust for your relative with a disability.

WHAT ARE THE BASIC THINGS I NEED TO THINK ABOUT? During the course of designing your Will and planning your estate you will need to:

- appoint an executor to ensure that the instructions in your Will are carried out

- divide your estate among family (spouse and children), charities, and others. A person who inherits or receives part of your estate is called a beneficiary
- create a trust—usually a discretionary trust—for your relative with a disability and identify a trustee and perhaps co-trustee to manage the trust
- appoint a guardian for your children who are under the age of 19 years.

If you die without a Will, you have no control over how your estate is divided.

WHAT HAPPENS IF I DIE WITHOUT A WILL? If you die without a Will, provincial laws set out how your estate will be distributed. Under the *Estate Administration Act* (BC), the court will appoint an administrator who will divide your estate. **This means you will have no control over how your estate is divided. You will not be able to protect the inheritance you want to leave to your relative with a disability.** The Public Guardian and Trustee holds your relative's inheritance until they turn 19 years, at which time they will receive their total inheritance outright. This situation may disqualify them from receiving BC disability assistance.

If you die without a Will and you have children who are under the age of 19—and there is no surviving parent who is the legal guardian—then the government will become guardian of those children.

HOW MUCH WILL MY CHILD WITH A DISABILITY GET IF I DIE WITHOUT A WILL? If you die without a Will, the *Estate Administration Act* directs:
- the first $65,000 of your property goes to your spouse—plus the household furnishings—and the right to live in the family home until death
- one third of the remainder of your estate goes to your spouse and the remaining two-thirds is divided equally among your children
- your next-of-kin will have to go to court to be allowed to deal with your estate

NOTE: For minor children, the OPGT becomes guardian of the estate whether you have a Will or not **unless** you have created a trust.

DOES THE *WILLS VARIATION ACT* MATTER TO ME? Yes it does. This Act requires that your Will provide adequately for your spouse and for your children. The definition of spouse in the Act includes an individual of either gender who has lived with and cohabitated with you for at least two years in a marriage-like relationship. If a spouse or children feel you have not provided adequately for them in your Will, then they can ask the court to change your will to get a larger share of the estate. This must be done within six months of probate.

If you do not leave your child with a disability (either an adult child or a minor) a fair share of your estate, it is likely the Public Guardian and Trustee will intervene on their behalf and try to change the Will.

WHO IS THE PUBLIC GUARDIAN AND TRUSTEE? The Public Guardian and Trustee is responsible for protecting the interests of both children who are under the age of 19 years and dependent adults. Your executor is required to send a copy of your Will to the Public Guardian and Trustee after you die if you have children under 19 or if you have children who are or may be mentally infirm. The Public Guardian and Trustee will examine the Will to see if you have made adequate provision for your children under 19 and any adult child with a disability. If you have not done so, the Public Guardian and Trustee may contest your Will on their behalf.

BC DISABILITY ASSISTANCE The BC Employment and Assistance is a provincial government program that provides financial assistance (BC disability assistance) as well as supplements such as medical, dental, optical, and pharmaceutical benefits to people with disabilities. To be eligible, a person must meet both the test for the Persons with Disabilities designation and the asset and income test.

Some people who do not qualify for BC disability assistance may qualify for income assistance as a person with Persistent Multiple Barriers; this type of assistance, however, provides somewhat fewer benefits.

A single person on BC disability assistance receives up to $906.42 per month for shelter and support while a single person receiving income assistance as a person with Persistent Multiple Barriers receives up to $657.92 per month. People on BC disability assistance can apply for an annual bus pass for $45 per year. People receiving income assistance as a person with Persistent Multiple Barriers are reassessed at least every two years for eligibility.

Once people are 18 years of age, they are entitled to BC disability assistance if:

- they qualify as a Person with Disabilities under the rules in the Employment and Assistance for Persons with Disabilities Act and Regulations
- they have less than $3,000 in assets; that is, things a person owns including money, property, and investments.

If an individual on BC disability assistance has assets of more than $3,000, they will be cut off until their assets are worth less than $3,000. **NOTE:** The RDSP is not considered an asset.

Individuals on BC disability assistance are entitled to be the beneficiary of a discretionary trust of any amount of money, an RDSP of any amount, or of a non-discretionary trust of up to $100,000 (and sometimes more), without being cut off. **NOTE:** the Minister responsible for BC disability assistance has the discretion to exempt an amount higher than the $100,000 if lifetime disability-related costs will be higher.

Individuals on BC disability assistance are also entitled to own certain exempt assets which don't count as part of the $3,000 limit. This includes a home they live in and a car they use. These are substantial benefits.

The *Employment and Assistance for Persons with Disabilities Act*, Regulations, and policies change from time to time. Check the Resources Section on page 187 for contact information or check the Ministry of Housing and Social Development's website for regular updates by visiting http://www.gov.bc.ca/hsd/. Scroll on the right to "Popular Topics" and click the Online Policy Resource Manual.

We don't have
to choose;
we have to
talk to each
other about
what concerns
us deeply.

HAROLD RHENISCH

HOW BC DISABILITY ASSISTANCE IS AFFECTED BY INCOME

EARNED INCOME

Persons on BC disability assistance are able to work and earn income. Each person is allowed to keep the first $500 of income without affecting their benefits.

UNEARNED INCOME

This is income from term deposits, bank interest, rental income, RRSPs, and so on, which has not been earned by working. Unearned income is deducted dollar for dollar from BC disability assistance. If a person receives $300 in unearned income, then their next month's payment will be reduced by $300. **NOTE:** Income from a RDSP is exempt from this provision.

HOW BC DISABILITY ASSISTANCE IS AFFECTED BY INCOME SUCH AS AN INHERITANCE If people on BC disability assistance receive income from an inheritance, a life insurance payout, an ICBC payout or other financial windfall, then they will be cut off BC disability assistance until they have only $3,000 left. If the person on disability assistance has the capacity to enter into a contract, then they can place up to $100,000 in a non-discretionary trust and up to $200,000 in an RDSP without affecting their BC disability assistance.

> **NOTE:** While there is a ceiling of $100,000 for non-discretionary trusts, there is no ceiling for discretionary trusts. That is why we strongly recommend you set up a discretionary trust. The non-discretionary trust can only protect $100,000 of the assets from an inheritance or settlement. Any trust can be set up during your lifetime or after your death; however, different income tax rules may apply. See below for the discussion on discretionary trusts.

WHAT BENEFITS DO MY RELATIVES QUALIFY FOR ONCE THEY TURN 65? When your relative reaches the age of 65, they will move from provincial income assistance to federal seniors benefits: Old Age Security (OAS) and Guaranteed Income Supplement (GIS). Together, these two benefits provide approximately the same amount as BC disability assistance.

I wear my shadows where they are harder to see, but they follow me everywhere. I guess that should tell me I'm traveling toward light.

BRUCE COCKBURN

Old Age Security is not asset or income tested. This means that all senior Canadians receive a monthly amount whether or not they have assets or income.

The Guaranteed Income Supplement is the federal government program that helps low-income seniors. It is not asset-tested; it is, however, income-tested. Any income that seniors receive is clawed back at 50 per cent including income from a discretionary trust.

The good news for holders of RDSPs is that the Guaranteed Income Supplement will not be affected by income received from a RDSP. In other words, RDSP income is exempt.

CAN I SET UP AN RDSP AND A DISCRETIONARY TRUST? Yes you can. There are benefits to each and you may want to do both. See page 145 for a comparison. In general, the RDSP is designed to build savings and can be used while parents are still alive. Discretionary trusts are typically designed to manage the inheritance you leave for your relative. A discretionary trust in your Will becomes operational only after you die. NOTE: If a grandparent sets up a discretionary trust, then the money may become available before the parent dies.

WHY SHOULD I SET UP A TRUST? A trust may be advisable for many reasons:

- to ensure the availability of ongoing government benefits such as BC disability assistance
- to help your relative with a disability during their lifetime and then to pass on funds that remain to another generation or a chosen charity
- to protect a vulnerable relative from being taken advantage of by those with bad motives and also those with good intentions but limited skills or judgment
- to provide ongoing financial management of assets
- to take advantage of special tax treatment
- to give some protection of assets if a relative goes through a marriage breakdown or has creditors.

Grandmothers should be ruling the world. I say this without a hint of a joke. Grandmothers see the future in a way others do not. As the world of the flesh decays, the life of the spirit flowers. Grandmothers are a field of wildly blooming exquisite and riotous flowers.

JOY KOGAWA

WHAT PROVISIONS SHOULD I ADD TO MY WILL TO BENEFIT MY RELATIVE WITH A DISABILITY? You can set up a trust in your Will for the person with a disability. The best course of action is to talk to a lawyer who has expertise in providing wills and estate advice to families of people with disabilities.

There are two common trusts used by families of people with disabilities: non-discretionary trusts (also called income trusts) and discretionary trusts.

NON-DISCRETIONARY TRUSTS

A non-discretionary trust can be set up in two ways. One way is by a friend or relative of the individual with a disability. The other way is by the individual with a disability.

Regardless of who sets up the trust, as long as the amount of money in the non-discretionary trust is under $100,000 it will not be treated as an asset for individuals on BC disability assistance. It's important to note that these trusts are reviewed by the provincial government and need to be designed properly in order to be approved. For example, there must be at least one trustee in addition to the beneficiary.

If the capital contribution to the non-discretionary trust is more than $100,000, then the individual will no longer be eligible for BC disability assistance unless the trust limit has been increased by the Minister of Housing and Social Development. Funds from the trust can be spent on disability-related costs without affecting the individual's entitlement to BC disability assistance.

A non-discretionary trust means that the beneficiary of the trust can request payment of funds out of the trust and the trustee has no discretion. **The trustee must pay out the requested fund.**

DISCRETIONARY TRUSTS

Most families of people with disabilities choose to set up a discretionary trust in their Will. To do this, you appoint a trustee—and possibly a co-trustee—as the person who will be in charge of the trust. You give the trustee the discretion, or power, to decide when and how much of the trust fund will be used from time to time for the beneficiary, in this

Lost and Found

Man finds gold.
Man loses gold.
Man finds time.
Man loses hair.
Man finds dream.
Man loses dream.
Man finds laughter.
Man loses time.
Man finds
meaning to life.
Man loses life.

TOM KONYVES

case your relative with a disability. Your trustee can then gauge your relative's changing needs over time and adjust disbursements accordingly.

HOW DOES A DISCRETIONARY TRUST AFFECT MY RELATIVE?

Most important, a discretionary trust allows the beneficiary to continue to receive BC disability assistance. The trustee(s) will buy your relative what is needed. The trustee(s)—not your relative—will decide how to spend money in the trust. That is why it is not considered your relative's asset. Decisions are made in someone else's discretion.

Under BC disability assistance, discretionary trusts are recognized as an exempt asset. There is no ceiling on the amount that can be placed in a discretionary trust. The trustee can use the trust for anything, but certain payments will be exempt from the unearned income rules including:

- medical aids and devices, renovations, education and training, cost of caregivers, and so on
- expenses of up to $5,484 a year that promote independence.

We are hopeful that these restrictions will be reduced to make them compatible with the RDSP. Check with PLAN to make sure you and your advisors have current information about these rules or check the Ministry of Housing and Social Development's website for regular updates by visiting http://www.gov.bc.ca/hsd/. Scroll on the right to "Popular Topics" and click the Online Policy Resource Manual.

WHAT HAPPENS TO THE MONEY LEFT IN THE TRUST WHEN THE BENEFICIARY DIES?

When you set up a trust, you must also identify who will get what is left in the trust when the beneficiary dies. This could be the beneficiary's spouse, children, siblings, other family members, charities or anyone else.

You should be careful to avoid a potential conflict of interest when you choose the trustees of the trust you establish for your family member. Who inherits the remainder of the trust? If the person inheriting the residual amount of the trust (the residual beneficiary) is the only person responsible for making spending decisions when the primary beneficiary dies, then there is a potential conflict of interest. One solution is to appoint co-trustees. We suggest you discuss this matter with your lawyer to avoid the Public Guardian and Trustee trying to vary the will.

WHAT DOES A TRUSTEE DO? The trustee:

- manages or looks after the trust assets
- makes sure your relative receives trust benefits according to your wishes.

If you decide to set up a trust for your relative, you will need to name the trustee in your Will. Choosing a trustee is one of the most crucial decisions you will make about future planning. The person you choose may have responsibilities as a trustee for 40 years or more.

It is a good idea to have more than one trustee. For example, you may want to have two trustees and two alternates in case the original trustees cannot act or cannot agree. It's also a good idea to choose a trustee who is much younger than you in age. You want them to live as long as your relative does!

WHO SHOULD BE A TRUSTEE? You may want to have one trustee with financial skills and a co-trustee who has a personal relationship with your relative. Their skill sets may be different and may complement each other. One trustee might make investment decisions, keep accounts, manage tax returns, and so on. The other trustee—a sibling or friend—would be in a better position to advise on how to spend trust funds.

You may consider using a respected trust company as one of the trustees. Some families use a trust company as one trustee and a relative or family friend as the other trustee. The trust company can make sure there is experienced financial help to invest and manage the trust assets. The relative, friend or Personal Network member makes sure the funds are spent in the best interests of your relative.

If you name a person as a trustee, then you should also name a successor in case the first person dies, moves or is otherwise not willing or able to continue. It is best if the trustees are people your relative knows and likes. The trustees and your relative will likely be involved with one another for a long time. A good relationship between them will benefit everyone.

At least one of the trustees should live close to your relative. If a trustee has close contact with your relative, they will understand the needs of your relative better.

WHAT ARE THE DUTIES OF A TRUSTEE? The duties of a trustee include:

- deciding how and when to spend funds
- making payments to or for the beneficiary
- managing investments and safekeeping assets
- coordinating any maintenance/repairs of real estate
- preparing trust tax returns
- maintaining records of the trust
- reporting to the beneficiary or Representative about the trust.

NOTE: you can direct your trustees to consider certain expenditures, for example to purchase a home for your relative.

IN BC DO EXECUTORS AND TRUSTEES GET PAID? You can state in your Will or in a contract how much your executor is to be compensated. If you don't say how much they should be paid, provincial laws set a fee. In British Columbia, executors can charge up to 5 per cent of the capital and income of the estate. Your beneficiaries or the court must approve the fee. The fees that trustees charge are determined by the amount of time, effort, and skill that has been required of them while acting as your trustee.

If your executor is also administering a trust, then they may claim an extra amount of up to 0.4 per cent of the average value of the assets in the trust each year. These amounts are set out in the *Trustee Act*.

WHAT INVESTMENT POWERS SHOULD I GIVE MY TRUSTEE?
Trustees are limited by law to investments that a prudent person would make. You may give them greater investment powers but you must specify it in your Will. Be sure to discuss this with your lawyer.

> Choosing a trustee is one of the most crucial decisions you will make about future planning.

CAN I APPOINT A GUARDIAN FOR MY CHILD IN MY WILL? If you have children under the age of 19, you should appoint a guardian for them in your Will. You should also appoint alternates in case the first is not able to accept. You can't appoint a guardian for an adult child even if they have a severe disability. Guardians for adults can only be appointed by a court and are called Committees (see page 92). Better still, assist your adult relative in developing a Representation Agreement (see page 87).

Where there's a Will, there's a way.

WHO SHOULD BE THE EXECUTOR OF MY WILL? The executor is the person who makes sure that the instructions in your Will are carried out after you die. Often people appoint their spouse as their executor, but you may need to appoint someone else or someone jointly with your spouse. You should also appoint alternates in the event the original executor is unable to fulfill the responsibilities of executor.

If you have set up a trust in your Will, usually the executor and alternate executor will be the same as your trustees and alternate trustees. However, in some cases—for example where there is business to be managed—you may wish to have different executors and trustees. Talk to your lawyer about this.

WHICH OF MY ASSETS DO NOT FORM PART OF MY ESTATE AND PASS OUTSIDE THE WILL? Any assets held in joint tenancy with another person pass directly to that person on your death and are not governed by your Will. For example, a home and bank accounts held in joint tenancy with your spouse go directly to your spouse on your death.

Life insurance policies with a designated beneficiary pass outside the will directly to that beneficiary.

RRSPs and RRIFs with a designated beneficiary pass directly to that beneficiary.

Quite often when a spouse dies, most of the family assets are held in one of these ways and pass directly to the surviving spouse. Assets which pass outside your Will save probate fees.

Assets held in trusts that have been established prior to your death are also not part of your estate.

Be sure to consult your lawyer about putting assets in joint tenancy with your children or anyone else as there are dangers as well as benefits in so doing.

SHOULD I MAKE A GIFT TO A CHARITY THROUGH MY WILL?

Estates often have a lot of taxes to pay. This is because any funds in RRSPs and RRIFs are considered income in the year of a person's death. Other assets are deemed to be sold in the year of the death. Tax is payable by the estate on this income and any earned capital gains. When you make a gift to a registered charity through your Will, your estate receives a charitable tax receipt which can be used to reduce the income tax that has to be paid.

If you have supported charities while you are alive, you may wish to consider supporting charities through your Will. You should discuss these wishes with your estate planning professionals. Most charities have planned giving programs set up to be able to respond to inquiries about leaving a charity a gift through your Will. You are also able to leave charities gifts of life insurance, property, RRSPs or RRIFs, as well as through many other innovative vehicles. When you have decided on your charity—or charities—of choice, you should consider contacting them to discuss the gift.

CAN I MAKE A GIFT TO PLAN IN MY WILL? Many families appreciate the work that PLAN does and support its continued financial independence by making a charitable gift or by leaving a bequest through their Will.

PLAN has established a Circle of Friends program to recognize and thank our major contributors. This is how it works: A professional journalist writes up each family's story which is then printed in our *Circle of Friends* book. This story is accompanied by a family portrait and a framed copy is provided to the family.

Please contact PLAN to discuss specific programs that you would like to support through your estate. Any request for anonymity will, of course, be respected.

To read a current story from PLAN's *Circle of Friends* book, please visit www.plan.ca and search for Circle of Friends.

SPECIAL TREATMENT FOR RRSPS AND RRIFS If you have a lot of assets in RRSPs or RRIFs, you may want to consider leaving them specifically for a son or daughter or grandchild with a disability when you die. If you do leave these assets to a child or grandchild with a disability, then the federal government provides a tax deduction equal to the total amount of the RRSP or RRIF going to that beneficiary. This means your estate wouldn't have to pay any taxes at all on these assets.

This can, however, create two problems. First, your relative may be vulnerable and, therefore, not able to manage that asset. Secondly, the asset will affect your relative's BC disability assistance. If the amount is less than $300,000, they may be able to put the funds into a non-discretionary trust ($100,000) and RDSP ($200,000) and not lose their BC disability assistance.

The federal government has indicated that they plan to permit funds from the RRSP or RIFF to be passed on to a trust but the legislation is not yet in force.

We recommend you discuss this option with your lawyer or check with PLAN for the most current information.

WHAT IS PROBATE? Probate is the name of the legal process that confirms your last Will. Normally it is the job of your executor to file your Will for probate with the provincial court and pay probate fees. This process can be up to six months. Until your executor receives the grant of probate, assets of your estate cannot be released.

Probate fees in B.C. are currently as follows:
- Under $25,000   No fee
- $25,000-$50,000 $6 for each $1,000
- Over $50,000 $14 for each $1,000

UNDER WHAT CIRCUMSTANCES SHOULD A PERSON WITH A DISABILITY SET UP A TRUST OR MAKE A WILL? Many individuals with disabilities do establish trusts and make wills. This will become even more important for people with RDSPs. The law has legal tests which all individuals—disabled or not—must meet in order to place their assets in a trust or execute a Will. For example, in order to create a Will, an individual must know what a Will is and know and understand what their assets and liabilities are and their value. If an individual cannot meet the legal tests required, then they would not be able to settle a trust or make a Will at that time.

An individual's capacity, however, is not a static thing. An individual without the legal capacity to execute a Will may, six months later, have the requisite capacity. Furthermore, lawyers vary in their understanding and appreciation of capacity of people with disabilities. You may find it useful to consult with legal professionals who have familiarity and experience working with individuals with disabilities. Please visit PLAN's website, www.plan.ca for a current list.

In some circumstances an individual on BC disability assistance may need to put part of their assets into a non-discretionary trust to remain on BC disability assistance. If the individual does not have capacity to create a trust, then a lawyer or advocate may be able to assist in finding another way to assist the individual to remain on BC disability assistance.

Seeking advice from professionals

There are a variety of experienced professionals in the future planning business. There is no substitute for good professional help. There are lawyers, financial planners, accountants, and trust companies who have special expertise in helping plan for the needs of children and relatives with disabilities. They can help you maximize the size of your estate, save you money, and ensure that your instructions are written in proper legal language. They are guided by principles of confidentiality, prudent administration, and sound judgment.

As with all professional services, be a cautious consumer. Always ask the professional their estimated fee before hiring them. Ask other parents or check with organizations such as PLAN. PLAN can provide some sample clauses that you may want to include in your Will and maintains an up to date list of qualified professionals.

The professionals you choose will be highly skilled but they still need the clarity of your vision to make the right plan for your family.

Questions to ask an advisor

When seeking advice on estate planning, tax planning, or wealth management strategies ask:

1. What is your experience, knowledge, and training?
2. How long have you been doing this?
3. How are you compensated for your advice?
4. Have you worked with other families who have a child with a disability?

Life changes

No matter how exhaustive your preparation and thorough your study, your Will may never be complete, will never be perfect. While preparing for this chapter, we were consulting with one of the most prestigious estate planners in the country. He interrupted our interview to visit his lawyer. After over 35 years in the business he is still revising his Will!

Expect to revise your Will as life changes. The act of revision is relatively painless and inexpensive. And the peace of mind is incalculable.

Eight tips in making your will if you have a relative with a disability

1. Complete the Will Planning Worksheet beginning on page 153. This will give you an idea of your assets and help you make decisions.

2. Decide how you want your estate distributed. For example: all to spouse and when spouse dies, split among children in equal shares.

3. Appoint an executor and alternate executor.

4. Decide if you want to set up a discretionary trust for your family member with a disability. Ensure there is no conflict of interest.
If you do, decide who will be:
- the trustee of the discretionary trust
- the beneficiary of the trust when your relative dies.

5. Be aware that the following pass outside the Will:
- life insurance with a designated beneficiary
- RRSPs and RRIFs with a designated beneficiary
- assets held in joint tenancy.

6. If you have children under 19 years of age, decide whom you will appoint as their guardian.

7. Take all this information to a lawyer who has experience in wills and estates for families and individuals with disabilities. Ask the lawyer to explain the tax and legal implications of your decisions. Also ask the lawyer about registering the Will with the Vital Statistics Agency, once it has been drawn up.

8. Discuss your draft Will with your trustees.

The new registered disability savings plan (RDSP)

Following more than eight years of federal advocacy by PLAN, Canada is the first country in the world to implement an RDSP. As a result, both the Government of Canada and the Government of British Columbia have now made it easier for families to secure the financial future of their relatives.

Canadian families now have a new resource to assist them to secure the financial well-being of their relative with a disability: the Registered Disability Savings Plan (RDSP). The RDSP will allow you to put funds aside for your relative and for those funds to grow tax-free. In most situations, the federal government will assist you by generously matching your contributions.

The RDSP is a tax-deferred savings plan for which as many as 500,000 Canadians with disabilities will be eligible. The RDSP is a new financial product that you can purchase from most financial institutions in Canada.

Maximum contributions to an RDSP are $200,000. There are no restrictions on the number of contributions you make. For example, you can make a large one-time contribution or you can make smaller contributions every year or some combination of lump sum and annual contributions.

Anyone can make a contribution: parents, grandparents, other family members, friends, agencies, foundations, and so on. The contributions are not tax-deductible and once contributed into the RDSP, they become the asset of the beneficiary.

When you make a contribution, the Canada Disability Savings Grant will add as much as three times your contribution to your relative's plan. How much, however, depends on your income or your relative's income if they are 19 years or older. If you earn under $75,769 a year, the matching is better (three to one up to a limit) than if you earn

> What a blessing
> it is that we
> can so dream
> into life the
> things we desire!
>
> LUCY MAUD MONTGOMERY

over $75,769 (one to one). Either way, the Canada Disability Savings Grant allows you to multiply your contribution and grow it tax-free.

In addition, once your relative turns 19—and assuming their income is under $21,287—they are eligible for the Canada Disability Savings Bond. The Canada Disability Savings Bond is worth $1,000 a year to a maximum of $20,000. If their income is between $21,287 and $37,885, then they can still receive a pro-rated portion of the Bond to a maximum of $20,000. When payments are made from the RDSP for your relative, the portion of the RDSP that is the Grant or the Bond—plus the accumulated interest—is taxable in the hands of your relative.

With the combined benefits of tax-free growth and compounded income, the RDSP will be a powerful planning tool for families. For example, if you have a nine year old daughter, you earn under $75,769 per year, and you contribute $1,500 annually to the RDSP for 20 years (total $1,500 x 20 = $30,000), she will have nearly $350,000 in savings by the time she turns 40. At that time, a life annuity could be purchased giving her an estimated $1,500 per month in additional income. For detailed examples of how the RDSP can work for your family, please refer to the scenarios on page 141.

The BC Government is the first provincial government to enable families to make full use of the RDSP. An RDSP is considered an exempt asset by the BC Employment and Assistance program. This means that a person can have any amount in an RDSP and still be entitled to receive their disability income and related benefits. Monies received from an RDSP are exempt from clawbacks against BC disability assistance. In other words, having an RDSP will not affect your relative's government benefits. In fact, a person can use RDSP funds at any time for any purpose without affecting their BC disability assistance.

Income from an RDSP is also exempt from clawbacks against the Guaranteed Income Supplement. This is important because once your family member turns 65 years of age, they move from BC disability assistance to the Old Age Security and Guaranteed Income Supplement. Currently, any outside income is clawed back—except payments from

For examples of how the RDSP can work for your family, please refer to the RDSP Scenarios on page 141.

an RDSP—from the Guaranteed Income Supplement at a rate of 50 per cent.

Both levels of government have sent a clear message to families: they trust people with disabilities and their families and there is no need to interfere with how families spend their money and how they live their lives.

Basic Elements of the new RDSP

Anyone eligible for the Disability Tax Credit (DTC) is eligible to open an RDSP. Qualification for the DTC requires a "severe and prolonged impairment." For details, see Income Tax Form T2201. To obtain a copy, please visit http://www.cra-arc.gc.ca/E/pbg/tf/t2201/ or call Canada Revenue Agency at 1-800-959-2221.

In addition to the RDSP, there is a companion Canada Disability Savings Grant and Canada Disability Savings Bond. These are detailed below.

> I wouldn't have seen it if I hadn't believed it.
>
> MARSHALL MCLUHAN

Features of the RDSP include:
- a lifetime contribution limit of $200,000 but no annual contribution limit
- contributions can be made by anyone or any organization including but not limited to: your relative, you or any other family member, a friend, or a foundation
- a person can only have one RDSP
- an RDSP can be opened at most financial institutions. For a current listing of financial institutions offering the RDSP please visit www.rdsp.com
- contributions to an RDSP can be made until the end of the year in which the person turns 59. Payments from the RDSP must begin once the person reaches the age of 60
- the RDSP grows tax-free
- the portion of the RDSP made up of government contributions and interest is taxed in the hands of the beneficiary; your contributions are not taxable when payments are made

- payments from the RDSP can begin at any time but if you have received the Grant or the Bond—to avoid penalties—payments should not begin until 10 years after the last Grant and Bond were received (see discussion on the Grant and the Bond below)
- lump-sum payments are permitted when family contributions exceed government contributions
- an RDSP can be moved from one financial institution to another
- an RDSP can be invested in most financial instruments; for example, T-bills, GICs, bonds, stocks, or mutual funds.

The Canada Disability Savings Grant

Features of the Canada Disability Savings Grant include:

- the amount of matching Grant or Bond your relative is eligible for depends on your net family income until they reach the age of 19 years, after which it depends on their income
- if your income or your relative's income is under $75,769, then the first $500 is matched 3 to 1; for example, $500 is matched by $1,500. The next $1,000 is matched 2 to 1; for example, $1,000 is matched by $2,000
- if your income is over $75,769, the first $1,000 is matched 1 to 1; for example, $1,000 is matched by another $1,000
- contributions may leverage matching federal Grants to a lifetime maximum of $70,000
- a person can receive the Grant until December 31 of the year in which they turn 49
- the maximum annual Grant is $3,500.

To avoid penalties, the Grant and Bond portion of the RDSP should be kept in for 10 years after you have stopped receiving them. For example, if you are making 20 years of contributions and your family member is receiving matching Grants and Bonds, then payments should not begin for 10 more years. This would be 30 years from opening the plan.

If payments from an RDSP are made within 10 years of receiving the Canada Disability Savings Grant or Bond, then any grant or bond received within the preceding ten years must be repaid.

If you set up an RDSP and decide you DO NOT want to receive the Canada Disability Savings Grant and the Canada Disability Savings Bond, then the 10-year rule referred to above does NOT apply to you. If you only receive family and friends contributions into the plan, then you will have no restrictions as to when payments can be made from the plan.

When your child is under the age of 19, **your** family net-adjusted income determines their eligibility for the matching Grant and Bond. Once they turn 19, it is **their** personal net-adjusted income that determines the size of the matching Grant and Bond.

Canada Disability Savings Bond

Features of the Canada Disability Savings Bond include:

- the Canada Disability Savings Bond will provide up to $1,000 per year to an RDSP for an adult whose income is under $21,287 per year
- children under the age of 19 whose family's income is under $21,287 per year are also eligible for the $1,000 Bond
- if the adult or family income is between $21,287 and $37,885, then they will be eligible for a Bond of a lesser amount
- the Bond is available to a lifetime total of $20,000
- a person may receive both the Grant and the Bond for a lifetime total of $90,000
- a person can receive the Bond until December 31 of the year in which they turn 49.

NOTE: The income thresholds of $75,769 for the Disability Savings Grant and $21,287 and $37,885 for the Disability Savings Bond respectively are indexed and will change over time. Please visit www.rdsp.com for updated information.

How to maximize your RDSP grants

If your income is under $75,769 a year:

- your first $500 will be matched by $1,500 from the Disability Savings Grant
- your next $1,000 will be matched by $2,000 from the Disability Savings Grant
- your $1,500 contribution—plus the matching $3,500 Grants—equals a total of $5,000 for your relative's RDSP.

If your income is over $75,769 a year:

- your first $1,000 will be matched by $1,000 from the Disability Savings Grant
- your $1,000 contribution plus matching $1,000 equals a total of $2,000 for your relative's RDSP.

Payments

Two types of payments can be made from an RDSP: Disability Assistance Payments and Lifetime Disability Assistance Payments.

Disability Assistance Payments can be of any amount at any time but are only permitted if family contributions exceed government contributions.

Lifetime Disability Assistance Payments are determined by a formula, which is approximately the amount in the RDSP divided by the beneficiary's life expectancy. It is possible to purchase an annuity with any amount of the RDSP. The annuity payments become part of the Lifetime Disability Assistance payments. These payments may begin any time but, once they begin, they must continue. Lifetime Disability Assistance Payments must begin in the year that the person turns 60.

Questions about the RDSP

Why should we open an RDSP if our relative is older?

The RDSP has a couple of advantages no matter how old your relative is. At age 65 people cease to receive BC disability assistance. Instead, they receive the Guaranteed Income Supplement (GIS). GIS income—including income from a discretionary trust—is clawed back at 50 per cent. Payments from an RDSP, however, are exempt. The RDSP is also able to grow tax-free while income in trusts is taxable. Therefore, even though your relative is older and they may not receive much, if any, of the Grant or Bond, it is still to their benefit to have an RDSP. It is important to remember than contributions can be made until December 31 of the year in which your relative turns 59.

What happens to my relative's RDSP when they die?

Assets in a person's RDSP become part of the person's estate and are distributed in accordance with their Will. If they don't have a Will, then their assets are distributed according to the *Estate Administration Act* (BC), Part 10–Distribution of Intestate Estate.

  If the individual dies after the 10-year waiting period, then the government Grant and Bond do not have to be returned. Any Grant or Bond must be returned, however, if the person dies before the 10-year period is over.

Who oversees my relative's RDSP?

The person who manages an RDSP is the holder. Parents are the holders and manage the RDSP when their child is a minor. When their child turns 19, they can become one of the holders. When a plan is opened for a person who is already 19 or older, that person must be a holder unless they assign the responsibility to a Representative or unless they have a Committee (see page 92 for more on Committees).

Tips to get the most out of your RDSP:

- start early
- contribute regularly
- maximize your Canada Disability Savings Grants
- remember that anyone can contribute to your relative's RDSP
- use PLAN's RDSP calculator to determine your best scenario. Visit www.plan.ca or www.rdsp.com and click on the RDSP calculator button.

What you need to do now!

- establish your relative's eligibility for the Disability Tax Credit (Income Tax Form T2201)
- file your Tax Return (or your relative's if they are 18 years or older) for the current and previous year
- ensure your relative has a Social Insurance Number number.

NOTE: We estimate that thousands of people in Canada are eligible for the Disability Tax Credit but do not apply because they have no income. Now they have good reason to apply because eligibility for the disability Tax Credit automatically makes your relative eligible for the Disability Savings Grant and Bond.

Before you buy an RDSP: three questions you might ask your financial institution

RDSPs may vary from one financial institution to another. Make sure your RDSP has the flexibility to meet unforeseen circumstances:

1. Does your RDSP permit Disability Assistance Payments (lump sum payments)?
2. Can you transfer your RDSP to another financial institution without penalty?
3. Are there penalties if you don't meet a contribution schedule?

The power of the RDSP

The following scenarios illustrate the potential of the RDSP. We have summarized our assumptions in each situation. Results will vary with different assumptions and your personal circumstances.

The RDSP and young children

Families with young children usually have a list of competing financial priorities. The RDSP represents an economical way for parents, grandparents—and perhaps other family members and friends—to put funds aside for your relative and, and by so doing, have the government contribute as well.

For example, if you have a four year old and are able to put aside $100 a month ($1,200 a year) for 20 years and your family income is under $75,769 your child will have over a quarter million dollars when they turn 34. In other words, your investment of $24,000 will multiply over ten times!

HERE'S HOW IT WORKS:

Family taxable income: under $75,769
Annual family contribution: $1,200 a year
Total family contributions from age 4 to 24:
$1,200 times 20 = $24,000
Matching Grant: $58,000
Bond: $6,000 (age 19 to 24)
Total Grant and Bond: $64,000

Value at age 34: $250,000 (approx.)
If Annual Lifetime Disability Assistance payments begin at age 34, then the first payment will be $5,200 and increase by 5.5% annually. Over $700,000 would be paid by the time your relative reaches the age of 65.

Alternatively, the funds could be withdrawn at a different age. For example:
Value at age 40: $360,000 (approx.)
Value at age 50: $640,000 (approx.)

There are an infinite number of combinations depending on how much you contribute and when. Please visit PLAN's RDSP calculator at www.rdsp.com.

Teens: Natalie

Natalie's squeals of satisfaction when a teammate scores a run are all the reward that her father, Eric, would ever ask for. "She loves being a part of the team and loves the excitement of the competition," says Eric.

While Natalie, like other teens, is focused on friends and fun, her mother Karin is aware of the uncertainty of the future. "When I close my eyes, I see us on the calm water above Niagara Falls. What's so frightening is that I don't know what comes next."

"The RDSP is a really concrete way to prepare for the future today. Financial security allows us to shape the future. We can begin to dream with it," adds Eric.

Karin is not currently working outside the home and Eric's income is under $75,769 so they will qualify for the maximum annual grant of $3,500. At 47 years of age, Natalie will be able to receive payments without any penalties and the plan will be worth about $350,000. It will pay her about $9,700 a year at the beginning and rise to $48,200 per year when she is 77 years old.

Karin and Eric think they can put aside $125 a month for an RDSP for a total of $1,500 per year. They plan to contribute for 20 years.

RDSP SUMMARY:

Natalie's age: 17 years

Family taxable income: under $75,769

Annual family contribution: $125 a month ($1,500 a year)

Family contributions from age 17 to 36: $30,000

Value of Grant: $70,000

Value of Bond: $18,000

Investments: moderate risk (estimated return 5.5%)

Age to begin receiving from the plan: 47 years

Approximate value of the RDSP when beginning payments (age 47): $350,000

Annual Lifetime Disability Assistance payments will approximately begin as follows:

$9,700 at age 47

$16,500 at age 57

$28,200 at age 67 and

$48,200 per year at age 77.

Transition to adulthood: Darren

Even in a crowded room Darren seeks out people standing alone, latches onto their arm and guides them into a conversation. It seems no one can refuse his broad smile.

"It's his gift," says his mom Janice, who keeps a watchful eye on him. "I'm not sure how he will put it to use after he finishes school in June," she sighs.

"I like the idea of the RDSP." she says, "I'm scared to death about the future. But as a single mom, I don't have much left to contribute after I pay the bills every month."

Janice plans to open an RDSP for Darren to get the Canada Disability Savings Bond. She's been to PLAN's Will and Estate Workshop and has counseled her elderly parents to put the share of their estate they plan to leave for Darren into a discretionary trust. If he's still young enough, the trust can make contributions to his RDSP. Otherwise, the trust can be used directly to secure his future.

RDSP SUMMARY:

Darren's age: 19 years

Taxable income: under $21,287 (determined by Darren's income)

Annual family contribution: $0

Value of Bond: $20,000

Investments: moderate risk (estimated return 5.5%)

Age to begin receiving from the plan: 49 years

Approximate value of the RDSP when beginning payments (age 49): $60,000

Annual Lifetime Disability Assistance payments will begin at: $1,750 and will rise by about $170 every year.

NOTE: The amount in the RDSP could also change if Darren's grandparents contribute to his RDSP.

Young adulthood: Maria

"I'm famous! I'm famous!" shouts Maria, surrounded by the cast of the Vancouver theatre production of Beauty and the Beast. She glows when she is speaking about musicals, the excitement palpable in her voice. If her parents George and Rosa had enough time (and money), this is where she would spend every evening.

Maria's parents are confident that they can provide a good life for her while they are alive and able. The RDSP provides the means for securing the future when they won't be around.

Rosa and George have a big extended family and, at the last big dinner, getting an RDSP started for Maria was a main topic of discussion. The family has set a goal of raising $25,000. George has no doubt it will happen. George and Rosa also plan to contribute $1,500 a year for 20 years.

RDSP SUMMARY:

Maria's age: 27 years

Taxable income: under $21,287 (determined by Maria's income)

Annual family contribution: $125 a month ($1,500 a year)

Total family contributions from age 27 to 46: $55,000 (annual contribution plus $25,000 lump sum amount)

Value of Grant: $70,000

Value of Bond: $20,000

Investments: moderate risk (estimated return 5.5%)

Age to begin receiving from the plan: 57 years

Approximate value of the RDSP when beginning payments (age 57): $475,000

If an annuity is bought, annual payments will begin at: $24,000 and will rise by an average of about $500 per year. Some or all of the funds in Maria's RDSP could also be used to help purchase a house or to deal with other requirements that may arise.

The future is here: Alex

Tom is a Lifetime Member of PLAN. Tom is confident that Alex's future is provided for. His Will is current and he directs his executor to establish a discretionary trust for his son, Alex. Alex also has a Personal Network.

Alex, who just turned 41, has many interests, including photography and volunteering. His extra time is divided between the local seniors centre and the food bank.

Tom knows that if he capitalizes on the Grant and Bond for the next eight years, Alex won't be able to access the plan without paying a penalty until he is 59 years old. Tom wants him to be able to start using it earlier so he is prepared to forgo the government contribution. What Tom likes is that it will earn interest—tax free now—and that Alex can use it for anything he wants without affecting his BC disability assistance. Tom also knows that—unlike a discretionary trust—Alex's RDSP will not affect his Guaranteed Income Supplement, which will replace his BC disability assistance once he turns 65 years old.

Tom's plan is to contribute $200,000 as soon as he can and then let it grow for about 10 years.

Tom will still set up a discretionary trust in his Will but the trustee will face more restrictions on spending than the holder of Alex's RDSP. The RDSP and trust combined, however, will provide a good life for Alex.

Tom's plan seems pretty sound. In 10 years, the $200,000 that he contributes will have grown to about $350,000. By purchasing a life annuity that is indexed for inflation at 2%, this will provide Alex with an annual income of about $16,000 per year at age 52, growing to about $29,000 when he is 83 years old, which is pretty good for a $200,000 investment!

RDSP SUMMARY:

Alex's age: 41 years

Taxable income: under $21,287

Family contributions at age 41: $200,000

Value of Grant: $3,500

Value of Bond: $1,000

Investments: moderate risk (estimated return 5.5%)

Age to begin receiving from the plan: 52 years

Approximate value of the RDSP when payments begin (age 52): $350,000

Life annuity: Approximately $16,000 per year, indexed at 2%.

Comparison – RDSP and Discretionary Trusts

Appreciating the differences between RDSPs and trusts will help you to determine which option is best for your family member. Some families may want to capitalize on the federal government matching RDSP grants; others may see trusts as a more viable option. Still others may want to do both. Please visit www.rdsp.com or speak with your qualified professional advisor for further assistance.

TRUST	RDSP
AGE	
You can establish a discretionary trust for a beneficiary of any age. Non-discretionary trusts can also be established at any age.	You can establish an RDSP for someone until the end of the year in which they turn 59. The Grant and Bond are only available until the end of the year in which the person turns 49. The younger a person is the more that person can benefit from the RDSP because: • they have more opportunity to use the matching federal Grant and Bond • the power of compounded income is increased • they can access the funds at a younger age without penalties.
CONTRIBUTION LIMITS	
There are no contribution limits on discretionary trusts. BC disability assistance is not affected by the size of the discretionary trust. BC disability assistance permits a maximum of $100,000 to be placed in a non-discretionary trust.	The RDSP has a $200,000 lifetime contribution limit. Combined with the maximum lifetime amount of $70,000 from the federal Grant and $20,000 from the federal Bond, the lifetime RDSP contribution maximum is $290,000.

TRUST	RDSP
CONTROL/DIRECTION	
The trustee(s) make decisions about investments and payments from a trust. They have absolute discretion to make these financial decisions if you establish a discretionary trust. Both trustee(s) and alternates can be identified in your Will when you set up the trust. You can also give trustees the power to designate alternates at a later date.	The holder(s) make decisions about investments and payments from an RDSP. Parents or legal guardians must be the holders of an RDSP established for a minor child. This role can carry on once the child becomes an adult. If an RDSP is established for an adult, then the adult must be one of the holders of the RDSP unless there is an appointed Representative or Committee (see page 92 for more on Committees).
INCENTIVES	
Setting up a trust for a relative with a disability is done entirely with private funds. Governments make no contributions nor offer any tax deductions.	The Federal government will contribute up to $90,000 through the Canada Disability Savings Grant ($70,000) and Disability Savings Bond ($20,000) to a RDSP.
ELIGIBILITY	
You can set up a discretionary trust to benefit anyone with a disability whether they receive BC disability assistance or not. For people receiving BC disability assistance, discretionary trusts are not considered an asset.	To be able to set up an RDSP, the beneficiary must be: • qualified for the Disability Tax Credit • younger than 60 years • a resident of Canada.
INVESTMENT	
Investment of assets in trusts is limited to prudent investor rules as outlined in the *Trustee Act* unless other investments are permitted in the Will.	RDSPs are limited to investments that qualify for an RRSP. There are few restrictions.

TRUST	RDSP
LIMITATIONS ON USE OF FUNDS	
Other than the general guidance or direction you give to your trustee(s), there are no limitations on how trustees can use funds from a trust to benefit the beneficiary. If the person receives BC disability assistance, then there are some limitations on how funds can be used without affecting BC disability assistance.	There are no limitations on how funds can be used. If the person receives BC disability assistance, then they are free to use funds from the RDSP for any purpose without affecting their BC disability assistance. Funds from an RDSP can be used any time but must begin to be paid to the beneficiary at age 60. There are some limitations on the amount that can be used from an RDSP if government contributions exceed family contributions.
TAX ON INCOME EARNED	
Trusts must pay taxes on income earned from investments. Income from a trust set up in your Will pays income tax at your relative with a disability's marginal tax rate. Income from *inter vivos* trusts are taxed at the highest marginal tax rate. There are some exceptions. Consult with PLAN or a lawyer for more details.	RDSPs are tax sheltered. Tax is not payable on investments while held by the plan.

TRUST	RDSP
TAX ON PAYMENTS	
No tax is payable when funds are spent from the trust.	Tax is payable on the portion of the payments that are made up of government contributions and interest earned in the RDSP. It is payable in the hands of the beneficiary; that is, at their marginal tax rate.
WHAT HAPPENS WHEN THE BENEFICIARY DIES?	
When you set up a trust, you identify who will receive the remaining assets when the beneficiary dies.	When the beneficiary of an RDSP dies, the RDSP becomes part of their estate and is distributed through their Will. If they don't have a Will, distribution is determined by the *Wills Administration Act* Part 10 – Distribution of Intestate Estate. **NOTE:** If the individual dies after the 10 year waiting period, the government Grant and Bond do not have to be returned. Some or all of the Grant and Bond must be returned, however, if the person dies before the 10 year period is over.

Worksheet 9 – Will planning for children and adults with disabilities

This worksheet will help you clarify your objectives in making a Will. The worksheet is located at the back of this section, on page 153. Take a look at it now. It is based on ones that all lawyers use. You can get a headstart by filling out this worksheet in detail. This way, you'll be better prepared for your meeting with your lawyer.

Resources

As you begin to draw up your Will, you will find our Wills, Trusts and Estates Seminars useful. We have developed this seminar to answer your questions about discretionary trusts, planning your Will, choosing an executor and guardians, and related issues. By the end of this seminar, you will be better prepared to have a lawyer draft your Will.

You can attend a seminar in person in the Lower Mainland, take the course on-line from anywhere in British Columbia or, if there is a group of you in your area, we'll bring the course to you. For more information, please visit www.plan.ca or call 604-439-9566.

If you want information on the RDSP, you can visit www.rdsp.com, where you will find the best—and most current—information in Canada. You will also find our RDSP Calculator and links to RDSP seminars, such as our free tele-learning courses.

Is your child under the age of 19?

If you have young children and you die without a Will, here's what happens.

ONE If there is a surviving spouse they get the first $65,000 of the estate, plus the household furnishings and the right to live in the family home until their death. Your estate will be divided according to the *Estate Administration Act*.

The remainder of the estate is divided as follows: one-third to the surviving spouse and the balance divided equally between any children.

The funds for your children will be held in trust by the Public Guardian and Trustee until your children reach the age of majority.

The surviving spouse will have to apply to the Public Guardian and Trustee's office to access the money held in trust for the use, maintenance and benefit of the child(ren). This holds true for day-to-day expenses as well as any special expenditures.

TWO If there is no surviving parent—that is, you both die—or there is no surviving parent who has legal custody, the Superintendent of Family and Child Services becomes the guardian of the person, and the Public Guardian and Trustee becomes guardian of their assets. In order for another relative or family friend to become guardian, they will have to apply to the BC Supreme Court.

To prevent a costly, complicated, and potentially messy and heartbreaking outcome, you must make a Will. If you have children under the age of 19, you must name a legal guardian for your child.

Demystifying definitions that could definitely derail you

BC Disability Assistance Financial support plus medical, dental and pharmaceutical benefits provided to people with disabilities in British Columbia.

Beneficiary A person to whom you leave things (money, gifts, insurance policy, RRSP, trust).

Bequest A gift of a specific item of personal property or a specific amount of cash identified in your Will.

Codicil A legal document used to amend portions of your original Will and requiring the same formalities of signing and witnessing needed for a Will.

Discretionary Trust A trust in which the choice as to how to spend the interest and principal is completely in the hands of the trustee.

Enduring Power of Attorney The power to conduct and manage your financial affairs even if you become incapable. See Power of Attorney.

Executor The person or professional named in the Will who is responsible for ensuring the wishes in your Will are carried out.

Grant of Probate Court order which is the executor's proof they can act as your executor.

Holder The person who administers an RDSP.

Intestate A person who dies intestate dies without a valid Will.

Inter Vivos Trust A trust that comes into effect during the lifetime of the person who established the trust. Also known as a Living Trust.

Life Interest Benefit given to someone in a Will which allows that person to have the use of the property or a certain sum of money only for the lifetime of that person. The remainder goes to someone else when the person with the life interest dies.

Non-Probatable Assets Assets that pass outside of the Will. For example joint tenant ownership of real estate and bank accounts, RRSP/RRIF, life insurance, and annuity beneficiaries.

Power of Attorney A written document giving someone else the authority to make financial and legal decisions on your behalf. Often used if you are going to be out of the country or want help in dealing with your financial affairs. See Enduring Power of Attorney.

Probate The procedure by which the Will of the deceased person is legally approved by the court and documented. It also confirms the appointment of your Executor.

Representation Agreement A written agreement in which you name a Representative(s) and give them authority to help you with your financial affairs and your health decisions.

Revocation Cancelling parts of or all of an existing Will.

Settlor The individual who establishes a trust.

Testator That's you, the person who makes the Will.

Testamentary Trust A trust set up in a Will that only takes effect after your death.

Trust A legal arrangement in which one person (the settlor) transfers legal title to a Trustee to manage the property for the benefit of a person (the beneficiary).

Trustee The person or company that manages the trust according to the instructions in the trust agreement or Will.

Worksheet 9

Will planning for individuals with disabilities

This worksheet is intended to:

- assist you in compiling information to take to your lawyer when you wish to make your Will
- assist in making you aware of decisions you will need to make and to help you make them.

After completing the worksheet you will be ready to contact a lawyer of your choice to make the Will. This worksheet does not give any legal advice. To draft a Will, you need to see a qualified lawyer.

A. Personal and Family Particulars

Date _____

1 Full Name _____

Address _____

Occupation _____

Home Phone _____ Office Phone _____

Date of Birth_____ Place of Birth _____

Citizenship _____

Marital Status (including plans to marry) _____

Date of Marriage_____ Place of Marriage _____

Do you have a marriage contract? _____

Have you or your spouse been married or lived in a common law relationship before?_____

2 Marriage or Common Law Relationship _____

Spouse's Full Name _____

Address _____

Occupation _____

Home Phone _____   Office Phone _____

Date of Birth_____   Place of Birth _____

Citizenship _____

3 Children (Please list all children of either spouse. Please note with a * any child of a former
marriage of either spouse and with ** any child with a disability. Please include children you
have adopted and children of any previous marriages or common law relationships.)

Full Name   Date of Birth

_____   _____

_____   _____

_____   _____

_____   _____

4 Other Dependents

Is there someone who is dependent upon you for financial support for whom you wish to provide, such as an elderly parent? _____

If yes, please complete the following:

Full Name _____

Address _____

Relationship _____

5 Other Responsibilities

Are you now serving as the Committee or other legal guardian for an adult who is disabled or incapacitated? _____

If yes, full name, address and relationship to you:

Full Name _____

Address _____

Relationship _____

Relationship to you _____

B. Will Particulars

1 **Appointment of Guardian(s) for Infant Children**

Do you have a child under the age of 19?

It is important to note that you CANNOT appoint a guardian for your disabled child who is older than 19.

Who will be their guardian(s) should you die before they reach age 19?

Name	Address	Relationship to you	Occupation

Who will be their alternate guardian(s) before they reach age 19?

Name	Address	Relationship to you	Occupation

2 Distribution of Your Estate

(a) Do you wish to leave your estate to your spouse if he/she survives you? _____

(b) Do you wish to share your estate between your spouse and your children? _____

 If so, how? _____

(c) If your spouse dies before you, do you wish to leave your estate to your children? _____

If so, in equal shares? _____

If in unequal shares, what proportion or amount is each child to get?_____

_____

(d) At what age do you wish your children to receive their share?_____

(e) If any child fails to survive to that age, do you wish his or her children to receive the share?

_____

(f) If one of your children dies before you do, who do you wish to receive his or her share of

your estate?_____

(g) If your spouse and children all die before you do, who do you want to receive

your estate?_____

3 Discretionary Trust for Someone on BC Disability Assistance

(a) Do you have a relative who is in receipt or likely in the future to be in receipt of BC disability assistance? ☐ Yes ☐ No

(b) Do you wish to set up a trust for this relative? ☐ Yes ☐ No

(c) Do you wish it to be a discretionary trust? ☐ Yes ☐ No

(d) Who do you wish to be trustees of this trust?

Name	Address	Relationship to you	Occupation

Note that you may have any number of co-trustees. You should discuss with your lawyer whether you want each trustee to be a co-trustee or an alternate trustee. You should also discuss with your lawyer the ability of your named trustees to appoint additional or successor trustees.

(e) Who do you wish to be alternate trustees if any of the ones you have named are unable to serve?

Name	Address	Relationship to you	Occupation

(f) Ultimate Beneficiary

When you set up a trust you must specify what happens to the assets left in the trust when the person whom the trust was set up for dies.

Who do you want to receive the assets left in the trust when the person for whom the trust was set up for dies?_____

Does this cause a conflict of interest? _____
You should make sure you discuss a potential conflict of interest with your lawyer.

(g) Trustee Powers

Do you wish your trustee to be able, if it becomes necessary or desirable, to buy, sell, rent, lease, or mortgage a residence for your relative with a disability?_____

If so, make sure you discuss your wishes with your lawyer. They will need to ensure they give the powers you want to your trustees.

Do you wish to give your trustees unrestricted investment powers to allow them to make any investment they think is appropriate? _____

      Or

Do you wish them to be restricted in what they can invest? _____

It is important to discuss with your lawyer the powers you wish to give to your trustees.

Do you want to leave a particular asset to a particular person? This includes clothing, jewelry, art, etc. If so, describe below. _____

_____

_____

Do you want to give a cash gift to anyone? If so, describe below.

_____

_____

_____

Do you want to give cash or another gift to charity? If so, describe below.

_____

_____

_____

You must be aware that some assets can pass outside of your Will.

Have you filed a description of beneficiary with the Plan Issuers for your:

a) RRSP   ☐ Yes   ☐ No

b) RRIF   ☐ Yes   ☐ No

c) Pension Plan   ☐ Yes   ☐ No

d) Life Insurance Policy   ☐ Yes   ☐ No

If so, these items will pass outside of your Will.

Do you own any other assets, for example property, bank accounts, etc. jointly with another person?   ☐ Yes   ☐ No

If so, these items will pass outside of your Will.

4 Additional Support for your relative

Do you wish PLAN to provide support for your relative when you are no longer able to do so? If so, contact PLAN to discuss incorporating appropriate clauses into your Will that will enable PLAN to assist your relative.

5 Other Comments or Instructions

_____

_____

_____

This is for additional information, which your lawyer might need to consider.

_____

_____

_____

C. Asset and Debt Summary

(please indicate if these assets or debts are not in British Columbia)

	Hers	His	Both
a) Cash and Term Deposits	$_____	$_____	$_____

b) Life Insurance

Insurance Co	Owner of Policy	Designated Beneficiary	Amount
_____	_____	_____	$_____
_____	_____	_____	$_____
_____	_____	_____	$_____

c) RRSPs

RRSP Institution	Owner of RRSP	Designated Beneficiary	Amount
_____	_____	_____	$_____
_____	_____	_____	$_____
_____	_____	_____	$_____

	Her name	His name	Joint Names
d) Stocks and Bonds	$_____	$_____	$_____
e) Pension Plans & Annuities	$_____	$_____	$_____

f) Describe any interests you may have in any proprietorships, partnerships or private companies. _____

g) Real Estate

	No.1	No.2
Address	_____	_____
Registered Owner(s)	_____	_____
Joint Tenants?	_____	_____
Estimated Value	$_____	$_____
Mortgage Balance (estimated)	$_____	$_____
Mortgage Life Insured?	☐ Yes ☐ No	☐ Yes ☐ No
Approximate equity	$_____	$_____

h) Personal Effects

Approximate value of household goods, furniture, jewelry, boats & automobiles: $_____

Are any of these articles owned jointly with someone else? ☐ Yes ☐ No

i) Miscellaneous

A) Interest in any existing estate or trusts: _____

B) Other substantial assets: _____

C) Do you have any real or personal property outside of British Columbia? If so, please specify. _____

D. Summary of Debts (other than mortgages previously noted)

Creditor	Life Insurance		Amount
_____	☐ Yes	☐ No	$_____
_____	☐ Yes	☐ No	$_____
_____	☐ Yes	☐ No	$_____

Estimated Net Value of Estate

	Her name	His name	Joint Names
Total Assets	_____	_____	_____
Less Total Debts	_____	_____	_____
Less Estimated Tax	_____	_____	_____
Liability	_____	_____	_____
Total Net Value of Estate	$_____	$_____	$_____

step six

securing your plan

Before my stroke, I had a mistaken notion that feminism meant independence; the unspoken corollary was that disability (and aging) meant shameful dependence on others.

What I have learned finally is that in asking for help I offer other people an opportunity for intimacy and collaboration. Whether I am asking for me personally or for disabled people generally, I give them the opportunity to be their most human.

In Judaism, we call this gift a mitzvah.

BONNIE SHERR KLEIN

Back seat driver

GEORGE HALL has seen the future and he likes what he sees. Sure he still has worries, but he is satisfied he has done everything he can think of to ensure Rick's future. What's more, he has seen Rick thrive in his new life. George has a real sense of what will happen when he's not around.

He has already started to take a back seat in his son's life. "I'm seventy-three next month," he exclaims. "I'm slowing down a bit. I guess I've earned the right to be a back-seat driver."

Besides, George has a backup. The chauffeur for all his plans is, no surprise, PLAN. He has become a Lifetime member of PLAN. PLAN is prepared to make a lifetime commitment to monitor the quality of Rick's life, to maintain the health of Rick's circle, to provide advice to his trustee, to visit Rick on a regular basis, and to stay on top of all the other plans George has made. In other words, all the things that parents do for their children now, PLAN is prepared to do after they're gone.

In this regard PLAN spells continuity as well as peace of mind to George. "It's better to make your arrangements with a group that you expect to be around for a while," he concludes.

But there's more. You see, while it's true that George's plans for Rick are focused on Rick's future, they are really about George's future as well.

George has sold the family home, leaving Rick behind while he makes a move to Sechelt on the Sunshine Coast. That's a move he never would have considered in the past.

George's wisdom is astute. "Part of the enrichment in life is learning. If you're feeling at all uncomfortable about your plans, a few simple steps will enhance the future for both you and your relative. You can't depend on anybody else, the government, the local association, your friends or family, on a loose arrangement."

As a former salmon fisheries biologist, George knows a lot about swimming upstream, about enhancement, about courage, and about destiny. It's time, he thinks, to complete the life cycle.

Besides you can't really qualify as a back-seat driver without having been in the driver's seat first. ∎

Securing your plan

Achieving a good life and a secure future for your relative requires careful attention to a number of key elements:

- a vision with as much detail as you, your relative, and close family and friends can muster
- the ongoing involvement of caring, committed friends and family
- control over the home environment
- appointed Representatives to assist with decision-making
- a properly drawn and executed Will
- a financial strategy including an RDSP and a discretionary trust
- sensitive and caring trustees who know your family member.

We trust you've also thought about:

- how you want to divide your property and financial assets
- which relative, friend, Personal Network member or company might be a trustee or co-trustee of the discretionary trust
- what services you may want from a lawyer, accountant, trust officer, and financial planner
- consolidating all this valuable information in the worksheets provided throughout this book!

We trust you now have a clear idea about what your relative's life will look like after you are gone. Your picture includes:

- who their friends will be
- where they might live
- how they will make their contribution to society
- what might be put in place to keep them safe
- who might serve as an advocate and monitor
- what role your other family members might play.

> The point of
> the journey
> is the
> transformation
> of the traveller.
>
> BRUCE RICE

Worksheet 10—Your Summary Checklist—can be found at the end of this step, on page 185.

Ode to David

A FEW WINTERS BACK David tripped and fell. Uncharacteristically, he seemed to be losing his balance regularly. Members of his Network accompanied him to a series of medical appointments only to hear the unimaginable: David had an inoperable brain tumor.

David's Network was told there wasn't much that could be done except to keep him comfortable and out of pain. In fact, a lot was done. His time in hospital precipitated an outpouring of love. The walls of his hospital room were papered with cards and banners. Amnesty International sent a poster listing all the campaigns David had participated in. The Vancouver Symphony made him a DVD. The Vancouver Bach Choir sent a video full of personal greetings. Political candidates for Mayor visited. At the hospital's request, David's Personal Network created a visitor's roster. It was becoming overwhelming for the nurses but not for David. More! I want more! was David's response.

David was aware of his condition while talking through all his options with his facilitator Karl and his closest friends. Routine mattered most. As Christmas was coming, friends arranged a larger than usual party. Sandwiches were cut to his specifications: crusts off, triangular shaped, with orange cake and sherbet for dessert. The conductor of the Bach Choir led the carols,

accompanied by the principal pianist of the Vancouver Symphony. Worried he might miss the chance to celebrate Mozart's birthday, David suggested the evening end with "Happy Birthday Dear Wolfgang!" "Yo Mo," was the refrain from a tattooed and pierced younger activist in attendance.

In time David moved into a hospice made more welcoming by the presence of a piano and a good sound system. Bramwell Tovey, the conductor of the Vancouver Symphony Orchestra, along with his wife Laura, visited just after David slipped into a coma. Speaking softly, Mr. Tovey thanked David for being the Symphony's number one fan:

You have visited me backstage after so many performances, always gracious, never gratuitous with your comments. Thank you for understanding what we were trying to do. Thank you for speaking the language of music. David, it's my turn to thank you. We love you.

Kissing David on the cheek, he left the room only to spot the piano. Soon Mozart's Masonic Funeral Music filled the room where David lay sleeping.

David rallied just two days before dying and insisted that his Network take him to the polling station to vote in the federal election—an engaged citizen to the end. David's death, when

continued on page 170

Families helping families

Your challenge is to make the necessary arrangements for your relative to have a safe, secure, and comfortable life beyond your lifetime. This is an immense challenge. Who knows what the future will be like? They haven't yet invented a cell phone that works from the grave but if they do the inventor will be a parent of a child with a disability! In the meantime, who can you count on?

If you are like us, you may still have one nagging concern: Who does what I do, keeping an eye on everything? Who will be my eyes and ears, my arms and legs? Who will monitor the plans I have made? What is my plan "B"?

Our answer is simple: trust other families in similar circumstances. PLAN was created so we could share our strength, expertise, and know-how. PLAN was created by a small group of families who wanted a new type of organization, one controlled by families, one that would remain financially independent, and one that would focus exclusively on the social and financial well-being of our relatives with disabilities.

PLAN offers four basic functions which correspond to the four letters in our name:

PLANNING FOR THE FUTURE We offer current information on everything you will need to plan for the future (and deal with the present for that matter). This includes information on:

- the new Registered Disability Savings Plan (RDSP)
- wills and estates
- trusts
- government benefits
- home ownership
- Representation Agreements
- disability tax benefits.

LIFETIME MEMBERSHIP We offer this for families who want PLAN as a back up to monitor all the plans they have put in place and to intervene and advocate where necessary.

PLAN
is
plan "B"

david's story

continued from page 168

it came, couldn't get any better: he died peacefully on the 250th anniversary of Mozart's birth.

Those who accompanied David on his final days couldn't help feeling that David's mother would have been pleased. David did not die alone as she feared. And his life, her life, was not in vain.

A memorial celebration was held at Fairview Baptist—a celebration which ended with more than 200 attendees singing ODE to JOY.

An Ode to a Good Life
An Ode to a Good Death
An Ode to Friendship
An Ode to David.

A Canadian Broadcasting Corporation TV documentary on David Cohen's remarkable life and death can be obtained through the PLAN Institute. Please visit www.planinstitute.ca. ■

ADVOCACY We offer both personal advocacy for individuals and families and public policy advocacy to improve the lives of all people with disabilities.

NETWORK We help you create and maintain a Personal Network for your family member.

Flowers and compost

When you think of it, our job description is much like a gardener's: to nurture, to hover, to be alert to changing conditions, to provide shelter from the storm, to fertilize where appropriate, to enjoy all stages of growth, to savour the beauty of the moment, and to appreciate the sweat of preparation. You learn a lot about life as a gardener. You learn, for instance, about the interrelationship between flowers and compost.

A beautiful rose that we have just cut and placed in our vase is very pure. It smells good, fresh, and fragrant. Rotting compost is the opposite.

But that is only if we look on the surface. If we look more closely, we will see that in five or six days the rose will become part of the compost. The truth is, we do not need to wait that long. We can see it now. Take a deep look at the rose. Can you see the compost in the rose? Take another look at the compost. Can you see the rose in the compost?

If you are a gardener, you recognize that you cannot have one without the other. The rose and the compost are equal. The compost is just as precious as the rose.

If you are a parent, you understand that much of the beauty you create arises out of life's darker moments or in response to threats on the horizon. It is also true for us as a movement of families.

The parent-based disability movement arose at the end of the Second World War in the wake of the eugenics movement and the atrocities committed against people with disabilities. It also arose in reaction to professional advice to send our children away to institutions. Those early seeds of change—planted in dank soil—have blossomed into the most wondrous of plants.

The parent-based disability movement was the first internationally-based consumer movement. It led to the creation of the UN Charter of Human Rights for Persons with Disabilities. Before Ralph Nader, before consumerism, we existed!

Looking into the future

We see some disturbing trends and new challenges on the horizon which we are paying close attention to. Think of these challenges as the weather conditions that any sensible gardener needs to prepare for. So let's descend underground into the compost and poke around for a while. Perhaps we'll see the seeds of a solution, the beginning of another beautiful plant!

CHANGING DEMOGRAPHICS Within 15 years, population aging will be a key challenge facing our national and provincial economies. In 2005, there were 44 children and seniors for every 100 Canadians of working age. By 2030, there will be 61 children and seniors. By 2025 there will be more people over 65 than under 15 in British Columbia.

The potential impact is threefold. One, there will be fewer taxpayers and therefore smaller operating budgets at every level of government.

Two, increased health care expenditures (one source suggests if current trends continue, health care costs in BC will account for more than 70% of the BC budget by 2017).

Three, with a smaller fiscal pie and a greater share of the smaller pie going to health costs, there will be fewer resources to respond to social, educational, and environmental challenges.

Not everyone agrees on the size of the fiscal challenge we face. Every expert has a different set of assumptions. Maybe health care costs won't rise as dramatically as predicted. Maybe a new wave of immigration will fuel our economy. Maybe our birth rate will stop declining. We can't predict how governments will respond and how successful they will be in reining in health costs, and creating more efficiencies.

We do think it is prudent, however, to recognize there may be less financial resources to spend on disability supports in the future.

There is something bigger than fact: the underlying spirit, all it stands for, the mood, the vastness, the wildness.

EMILY CARR

NEW WORTHINESS DEBATE Relatives, friends, and supporters of vulnerable people are constantly reminded of how fragile society's support for people with disabilities can be. Debates about mercy killing, right to die legislation, and a reverence for technology and genetic engineering reflect a quest for perfection and implicitly a belief that some lives are not worth living. With every new tragedy or scientific discovery, fears surface that ambiguous terms like "quality of life" will be used within an emerging "new" eugenics movement. In the past, funding shortfalls have been linked to cutbacks in support for people deemed not as worthy; that is, because they are not contributors or productive and, therefore, are a drain on society's limited resources. Our challenge is to ensure our relatives with disabilities will have fair access to future medical treatment and other government funded supports.

New solutions for changing times

Fortunately families are used to turning adversity around. Reduced tax bases, and the increasing size of health care budgets are just the latest in a series of challenges we have faced before. We are confident the natural ingenuity and creativity of families will lead to new solutions for our changing times. PLAN is one of them.

Planned Lifetime Advocacy Network

The families who created PLAN had a clear list of do's and don'ts. Do create an organization that can withstand the winds of change. Don't rely on government funding. Do become financially self-sufficient. Don't do anything to weaken your effectiveness as advocates and monitors.

These families wanted an organization that would survive them. That would not drift from its mission in a search for funding. That would keep an independent eye on all the plans they had made for their individual relatives as well as for all persons with disabilities.

Here are the core values, concepts, and approaches that embody the PLAN model.

PLAN's core values

Our founding parents lived through decades of changes affecting their relatives. Many of them created the original parent-led community living and disability organizations. They had experienced the ups and downs of government funding. They knew the quality of programs and services could vary. They knew what to avoid and what to emphasize. They wanted to create a positive organization based on a spirit of abundance.

They built our organization around four core values:

1. Relationships keep people safe and are the foundation of a good life
2. Financial self-sufficiency—no reliance on government funding for organizational operating costs
3. Family leadership—our constitution calls for a majority of board members to be family members
4. Contributing Citizenship—the contributions of our relatives leads to their recognition as full citizens and brings meaning to their lives.

PLAN's four basic functions:

FUTURE PLANNING ADVISORY SERVICE

PLAN offers up-to-date information on all the elements of future planning. Through family visits, workshops, telephone referral, kits, newsletters, e-zines, videos, and personal contact, PLAN provides families and individuals with disabilities with, for example:

- the latest information on preparing a Will and planning an estate, disability tax benefits, and the new RDSP
- referrals to professionals sensitive to the unique issues a relative with a disability presents
- advice on preserving your relative's government benefits
- sample Will clauses

- information on Representation Agreements
- a home ownership advisory service.

CREATING AND MAINTAINING A PERSONAL NETWORK

PLAN believes the best time to consolidate friends and family into a Personal Network of support is NOW. PLAN's future involvement in the life of a person with a disability is conditional upon the existence of a Personal Network and PLAN's active involvement with the individual, the Personal Network, and the family. Without this personal and intimate contact with people and their families, PLAN would not be in a position to understand—let alone advocate for—the best interests of the person with a disability.

PLAN will create and develop a Personal Network for people upon request.

FAMILY SUPPORT AND ADVOCACY

A common response from families associated with PLAN is the degree of support and comfort they derive from working together. "This is just like the old days," is an often heard comment. PLAN's program is based on family to family contact. Families co-present with professionals at all workshops. Families make personal visits to other families. Families with Personal Networks meet regularly to share concerns and to seek advice from each other. Families accompany each other to critical meetings as advocates.

On a broader scale, PLAN works closely with provincial and federal governments to advocate for legal and financial improvements that will benefit people with disabilities.

> A social enterprise fulfills its mission by earning its income. It also sits on untapped resources which can be mobilized for social good.

Two ways to join PLAN

1. Become an Associate and get our regular newsletters, e-zines, publications; attend our workshops; support our ongoing policy work.
2. Become a Lifetime Member and work with us to develop a Personal Network for your family member.

This is the ultimate and most fundamental function of PLAN. Families can take advantage of all the services offered by PLAN. However, if you want PLAN to watch over and protect the best interests of your relatives after they die, then you must become a lifetime member.

A PLAN membership means we commit to overseeing and ensuring that the future plans you have made are carried out. PLAN becomes the foundation on which you can rest all your other plans. PLAN is another check in the system of checks and balances we recommend you set up for your relative.

For example, lifetime members can expect PLAN to:

- assist and advise their trust and trustees on decisions for the benefit of their relatives
- maintain the health of their relative's Personal Network
- visit their relative on a regular basis
- monitor the services they receive
- advocate for changes that will protect or improve their relative's quality of life
- carry out any specific wishes
- respond to emergencies and crises
- oversee the housing arrangements they have made
- oversee Representation Agreements
- protect and improve laws and policies.

PLAN's social audit: staying faithful to our values

Our social audit measures member satisfaction and our effectiveness at achieving our goals. It gathers input from our individual and family members, Personal Networks, staff, business partners, and community supporters.

If you would like to read what families have to say about PLAN check out www.plan.ca or www.socialaudit.ca.

PLAN: a social enterprise

If you are interested in learning more about social enterprise and social finance, please visit www. planinstitute.ca and click on Innovate with Us.

Since our founding parents did not want us to rely on government funding, we became a social enterprise. A social enterprise is a new type of not-for-profit organization that fulfills its social mission by earning its income. Social enterprises realize they sit on untapped resources which can be mobilized for social good.

Our expertise was detailed knowledge about what parents and families needed in order to create a safe and secure future for their relatives. This brought us in touch with credit unions, banks, life insurance companies, law firms, and financial and estate planning advisors who were interested in catering to this emerging segment of the disability market.

Our social enterprise revenue sources include:

- partnering with law firms, financial institutions, and companies who are in the future planning business
- charging a fee for our products and services.

Our emergence as a social enterprise has not been without struggle. It was a difficult decision to charge for our services. But we knew without financial independence our effectiveness as advocates was limited. We now have an Endowment Fund to assist those who cannot afford to pay our nominal fees.

There are many benefits to being a social enterprise. It has enabled us to stay faithful to our core values. We are able to use our new found economic muscle to further our social objectives. Our diverse funding base has made us more stable financially. The money we earn doesn't come with strings attached. This flexibility enables us to respond to emerging needs such as, for example, launching the campaign to create the RDSP.

Perhaps more importantly, being a social enterprise allows us to earn our own way. We are confident this independent economic base prepares us for whatever the future holds and is a model for other organizations to follow.

PLAN: building a policy foundation for the future

We learned an important organizational lesson in PLAN's early years. Our innovative programs would not have much impact unless they were recognized by society's systems and institutions. We needed our governments to recognize and adjust their regulations, policies, and statutes to accommodate the solutions we were developing. Since then, we have learned that all social innovations require corresponding structural changes in order to be sustainable, long lasting, and to have widespread impact.

Examples of our public policy advocacy include:

- co-founding the coalition to reform Adult Guardianship legislation and introducing Representation Agreements. Representation Agreements provide status to families and members of Personal Networks to support people with disabilities make decisions;
- PLAN proposed, researched, financed, and led the campaign to establish the world's first disability savings plan, the new RDSP. We worked with the Province of British Columbia and other provinces to accommodate the RDSP by raising asset limits and eliminating clawbacks from provincial disability benefits regulations;
- convincing the federal government to allow RRSPs and RRIFs to be transferred into a discretionary trust or RDSP for a child or grandchild with a disability;
- making discretionary trusts easier to use by expanding allowable expenditures and reducing reporting requirements;
- creating a new category of non-discretionary trusts to protect funds up to $100,000.

These accomplishments are laying the foundation for a new approach to disability–one that moves away from welfare thinking to one that acknowledges the contributions of families and provides them with better tools to secure the future.

We are convinced our effectiveness as individual advocates and public policy advocates is partially due to our financial independence from government. We are free to determine our priorities and are able to work with government as equal partners without fear they will withdraw funding.

The emerging disability market

Most of us have heard about the green economy—businesses dedicated to reducing pollution and lightening our ecological footprint. Perhaps you have heard of the grey dollar, that is, products and services purchased by seniors. Or pink tourism—businesses catering to travel by gays and lesbians. These are all markets that have grabbed the attention of businesses and companies.

As we developed and matured as a social enterprise we discovered there was also a disability market. One of the most promising areas for the future of the disability sector is to mobilize this market to assist with our financial sustainability. For example, the estimated RDSP market in Canada is at least $80 billion. The discretionary trust market size is another $80 billion. $160 billion is a lot of money! Can you think of ways we can mobilize our collective economic wealth to protect the future of people with disabilities? We can.

Some of our ideas include pooling the capital in our RDSPs and discretionary trusts to create a Disability Investment Fund. Another idea is to establish a No One Alone Fund to finance the costs of social networks. We are convinced that harnessing our collective economic power is a critical component in securing the future for all people with disabilities. Contact PLAN if you are interested in pursuing any of these initiatives.

Helping families around the world

PLAN Institute for Caring Citizenship

To respond to the growing interest in PLAN from across Canada and around the world, we created the PLAN Institute.

The PLAN Institute:

- provides on-line courses, workshops, training, and consultation on caring citizenship; social network facilitation; social enterprise; family leadership; organizational development; and social innovation
- mentors groups of families who are adapting the PLAN model
- distributes books, CD ROM's, and DVD's
- researches and publishes on citizenship, social networks, and belonging.

The Institute currently supports over 40 replications around the world. It offers an annual Leadership Training course for people interested in learning about the PLAN model. For those interested in learning about social movements, the Institute offers a four day retreat called Thinking Like a Movement, which takes place every January. For more information about the PLAN Institute visit: www.planinstitute.ca.

Wherever you live, we can help

No matter where you live in British Columbia we can help you put your plans for the future together.

We will travel to your community to present workshops.

PLAN and PLAN Institute offer on-line courses that are available at convenient times.

Our professional referral list includes lawyers and estate planning professionals from around the province.

We are connected to local groups who may be able to assist you in developing a Personal Network for your relative.

We are as close as a phone call or an email.

Philia dialogue on caring citizenship

When we think of citizenship, we usually think of rights and responsibilities. There is an expectation that everyone in society has a responsibility to contribute. Our friends and family members want to contribute. They are an under-utilized resource in society. We believe the next advance for people with disabilities will be made from this theoretical foundation. To promote these ideas, we created an inter–national web dialogue on caring citizenship. Please visit www.philia.ca.

PLAN: A model for creative problem-solving by families

PLAN is an organization providing hands on, practical support to families and people with disabilities. It is also a movement of families.

In the broadest sense, PLAN is about:

- strengthening the family arm of the disability movement
- working together on behalf of all our family members with disabilities
- welcoming supporters from all sectors of society
- focusing on the abilities of ourselves, our relatives, and our neighbours
- seeing the possibilities by creating a climate of continuous innovation
- meeting government as an equal
- putting all our eggs in one basket and treating them gently
- finding roses in the compost.

We were struck recently by a comment from one of our founding members, Joan. She pioneered the development of services and programs for many people with disabilities and has been a long-time advocate for families. "I'm having so much fun," she said. "It reminds me of the early days of the parent movement. Everything is so positive. Rather than tearing down, we are constructing something new. It so much easier to get things done. So much more satisfying."

Achieving the complete Personal Future Plan

This workbook has presented six steps for preparing for the future—and indeed changing the present—for your relative:

STEP ONE – CLARIFYING YOUR VISION

Rallying people around your hopes for the future.

STEP TWO – NURTURING FRIENDSHIP

Creating and maintaining a strong network of caring, committed friends and supporters.

STEP THREE – CREATING A HOME

Making a house a home.

STEP FOUR – MAKING SOUND DECISIONS

Protecting vulnerabilities and honouring choices.

STEP FIVE – ACHIEVING FINANCIAL SECURITY

Wills, trusts, and the new RDSP: Using all the legal and financial tools at your disposal.

STEP SIX – SECURING YOUR PLAN

Appointing and mentoring your replacements whether they are individuals or organizations like PLAN.

As you have seen, each step builds on the last one. Each one on its own advances the opportunity for greater safety and a better life. The steps are also interrelated and, taken together, they offer a complete system of checks and balances. They may not be foolproof but they are thorough. And that's what is needed to replace what families do now and to provide continuity from one generation to the next.

No one, not even those who have been involved in the future planning business for decades, is ever satisfied with their final product. There will always be tinkering and adjusting. That's natural. The difference is you will be amending a plan that is already in place. The hard work will already have been done and the basics will have been covered.

We can assure you the results will lead to peace of mind.

Advice for parents of younger children

Parents with younger children are faced with enough daunting challenges: being first time parents, dealing with the news of a child's disability, and responding to additional health challenges. We know this can be a tumultuous and intense period. You may not wish to focus on the future. We understand.

Perhaps the best resource we can offer is our Warm Bear program. Your child gets a warm cuddly bear and you get some basic information and practical tips on where to start. More important, you get linked into a network of supportive parents who have faced the same challenges.

Here are some additional tips:

- Grandparents can help in a variety of ways including making contributions to your child's RDSP or leaving money in their estate to create a discretionary trust.
- Life insurance can be an affordable way to finance a trust. You control the monthly payments and, should you die, the proceeds finance a discretionary trust for your child.
- Don't hesitate to invite friends into your child's life. Keep track of everyone who is friends with your child. You will be pleasantly surprised at how many of these people will become Personal Network members when the time comes.
- After high school is a good time to begin organizing a social network for your teenage child.
- Remember to create a Will and indicate who you want to become guardian of your children. Step Four outlines what happens if you don't.
- Connecting with other parents who have children with disabilities is the single best support for any of the tough decisions you will have to make on behalf of your child.

Conclusion

Safe and Secure is a workbook for gardeners. We have supplied you with the seeds of inspiration and information. But it is up to you to supply the rest—the planting, the weeding, the watering, and the nurturing. We are confident your shovel and hoe will dig a path into new territory. You will make the rows boldly and follow them fearfully. You will go where the rows lead. At the end you will have created your garden. In your hands your garden will have flourished. It will have become a place of security and repose.

We have supplied the seeds. You supply the love.

In concluding this book we wanted to end with a final story that would motivate or inspire you to march right out and do everything that needs to be done. The truth is, we've already written everything we know. We've nothing left to say. No final flourish. We're still in the field ourselves, you see. Look around you. There we are, your companion gardeners. ■

Warm Bear Program

PLAN has been providing a cozy bear to children with disabilities since 2000. Recently, this program has become available to families around British Columbia, thanks to support from Variety, the Children's Charity of BC, and Warm Buddy Co. Interested families can contact inquiries@plan.ca to receive a FREE* package.

Package includes (over $100 in value):
- Warm Bear plush friend
- Copy of *A Good Life*
- Copy of *Safe and Secure*
- One-year Associate of PLAN
- One-year membership to Family Support Institute
- Additional family resources and information.

*If shipping is required, there is a $10 fee.

Worksheet 10

Your summary checklist

I have completed all the following documents:

☐ A family portrait of my relative.

☐ My letter to the future, clarifying my wishes.

☐ A list of my relative's documents: birth certificate, social insurance card, health care card, etc.

☐ An up-to-date Will that reflects my current wishes.

☐ A description of the purpose of the discretionary trust.

☐ An up-to-date list of my major assets and where they are kept (insurance policies, bank accounts, stocks, mutual funds, and so on).

and

☐ I have stored all these documents in a safe place.

☐ My executor knows where these documents are kept.

RESOURCES

Reading List

Becoming Human
Jean Vanier

House of Anansi Press Limited, 1998
We could have chosen any number of Jean Vanier's books because they are all worth reading. This book is illustrative of the power of Jean's insight which is inspired by people with disabilities.

The Body Silent
Robert F. Murphy

New York: W. W. Norton, 1990
Without a doubt this is one of the best books written about and by people with disabilities. An anthropologist writes about his own gradual experience of becoming a person with a disability and what keeps him safe and maintains his quality of life.

Breaking Bread and Nourishing Connections: People with and Without Disabilities Together at Mealtime
Karin Melberg Schwier and
Erin Schwier Stewart

Paul H. Brookes Publishing Co. Baltimore, 2005
A feast of insight into the art of dining and hospitality.

Building Communities from the Inside Out: a Path Towards Finding and Mobilizing a Community's Assets
John McKnight and John Kretzmann

We continue to model our work at PLAN on John McKnight's analysis and insights. You can download a pdf copy by searching Google for this title.

The Careless Society
John McKnight

New York: Basic Books, 1995
This represents the best of John's writing. Inspired by the CBC radio series, "Community and Its Counterfeits." John and his writings are a major inspiration to Al Etmanski.

The Church of 80% Sincerity
David Roche

A Perigee Book, New York, 2008
This is a funny, honest, and irresistible glimpse into everyone's inner beauty and worth.

Community: The Structure of Belonging
Peter Block

Berret-Koehler Publishers, Inc.; San Francisco, 2008
Peter eloquently and elegantly explains how belonging is the path by which communities can emerge out of fragmentation.

In the Company of Others
Claude Whitmyer, editor
Revised by Cathy Ludlum and the
Communitas Team

New York: Jeremy Tarcher, 1993
This is a compilation of writings on the art of community development and building community connections.

The Company of Others: Stories of Belonging
Sandra Shields and David Campion

Vancouver, The PLAN Institute, 2005

Crossing The River: Creating a Conceptual Revolution in Community and Disability

David Schwartz

Cambridge, Mass.: Brookline Books, 1992
The best description from an American point of view on the new way of thinking–or the paradigm shift–in social services for people with disabilities.

The Diving Bell and the Butterfly

Jean-Dominique Bauby

London, Fourth Estate, 1997
Recently made into a compelling and thoughtful movie.

Down Stairs That Are Never Your Own: Supporting People with Developmental Disabilities in Their Own Homes

John O'Brien and Connie Lyle O'Brien

Visit http://thechip.syr.edu.rsa.htm.
This is a good overview of alternatives to group homes and the conceptual shift that will be required in order to achieve widespread home ownership or rental accommodation for people with disabilities.

Facing Death, Embracing Life

David Kuhl, M.D.

Doubleday Canada, 2006
A sensitive and all encompassing guide for those living with a terminal illness and for those who care about them.

From Behind The Piano—The Building of Judith Snow's Unique Circle of Friends

Jack Pearpoint

Toronto: Inclusion Press, 1990
This is the book to read if you want to learn more about Judith Snow, an amazing human being.

Getting to Maybe: How the World is Changed

Frances Westley, Brenda Zimmerman, and Michael Patton

Toronto, Random House, 2006
PLAN's story is one of many used to illustrate a new approach to changing the world.

The Healing Web—Social Networks and Human Survival

Marc Pilisak and Susan Hillier Parks

University Press of New England, 1986
This book will give you all the theory behind the importance of social networks. In our opinion, it is a classic and a must read for anyone who wants to dig a bit deeper.

How to Change the World—Social Entrepreneurs and Power of New Ideas

David Bornstein

New York, Oxford University Press, 2004
This book tells the stories of people who have both changed lives and found ways to change the world.

How to Create a Trust

Visit www.vcpgv.org
This best seller is published by the Voice of the Cerebral Palsied. Already in its third edition, this popular resource guide contains updated information and a brand new section on Disability Tax Credits.

Mind/Body Health: The Effects of Attitudes, Emotions and Relationships (3rd Edition)

Keith J. Karren, Brent Q. Hafen, Kathryn J. Frandsen, Lee Smith

This is a very good book for introducing body/mind health issues.

Moving Toward Citizenship: A Study of Individualized Funding in Ontario
John Lord

Toronto, Individualized Funding Coalition of Ontario, 2006.

The Myth of Ability
The End of Ignorance
John Mighton

Vintage Canada, Toronto

John's writing honours and applies to every child. He pays attention to how kids pay attention, captures their imagination, and enlarges their self-confidence.

On Equilibrium
John Ralston Saul

Toronto, Penguin Books, 2001

John is PLAN's Patron, collaborator, and intellectual inspiration. The sections on Imagination and Intuition are thoughtful; they validate what formal systems ignore or discard.

One Candle Power—Seven Principles that Enhance the Lives of People with Disabilities and their Communities
Pat Beeman, George Ducharme, and Beth Mount's original work on Circles brought together, revised, and updated.

Toronto: Inclusion Press, www.inclusion.com. A classic!

PATH: Planning Possible Positive Futures
Marsha Forest, Jack Pearpoint, and John O'Brien

Toronto: Inclusion Press, www.inclusion.com. We like this one a lot. It's a practical planning process that provides a good way of stepping out of the day-to-day and allowing your heart and mind to soar. It also provides an excellent structure for strategic and future planning. Visit www.inclusion.com.

Pathways to Inclusion: Building a New Story with People and Community
John Lord and Peggie Hutchison

Concord Ontario, Captus Press, 2007

This is an examination of various perspectives on disability. John and Peggie provide insightful discussion on the current need for social innovation to move vulnerable citizens from areas of exclusion to social inclusion.

Peace Begins With Me
Ted Kuntz

Coquitlam, 2005

Ted is a Past President of PLAN. This best selling book inspires people from all around the world. Visit www.peacebeginswithme.ca.

Roots of Empathy—Changing the World Child by Child
Mary Gordon

Thomas Allen Publishers, Toronto, 2005

Mary is a spirited colleague whose work brings babies into classrooms to foster empathy, reduce aggression, and increase tolerance.

Slow Dance: A Story of Stroke, Love and Disability
Bonnie Sherr Klein

Toronto, Knopf Canada 1998

What's Really Worth Doing and How To Do It—A Book for People Who Love Someone Labelled Disabled

Judith Snow

Toronto: Inclusion Press, 1994
Words of wisdom and inspiration from one of the wisest.

The World we Want—Virtue, Vice and The Good Citizen

Mark Kingwell

Toronto, Viking, 2000.
Mark's writing on justice provides a thoughtful framework for a new theory of citizenship that includes people with disabilities and others whose contributions have been ignored.

Films and Videos

Best Boy

Ira Wohl

This film won an academy award several years back. It's a true story in which the director filmed the process of his cousin, a middle-aged man with a disability, leaving home. There is a companion follow-up documentary as well. You can find it at specialty video stores or libraries.

SHAMELESS: the Art of Disability

A film by Bonnie Sherr Klein

Art, activism, and disability are the starting point for what unfolds as a funny and intimate portrait of five surprising individuals.

The Ties That Bind

Force Four Entertainment Inc.
National Film Board of Canada, 2006

A documentary film about Chris Jordan, his family, and PLAN. There is a companion resource guide in both English and French. This DVD is for all families worried about the future well-being of their relatives with disabilities.

And Then Came John—The Story of John McGough

A video by Telesis Productions, Mendocino, California

This remains one of our favorites. It's a true story of an artist, who happens to have Down syndrome, and the love that emanates from his connections in the community.

Our collaborators

www.2010LegaciesNow.com This website promotes full inclusion and accessibility in association with 2010 Vancouver/Whistler Paralympic and Olympic Games.

www.abilities.ca This is the website for the talented Ray Cohen's many important initiatives including Access Guide Canada and the award winning *Abilities* magazine.

www.ashoka.ca This is a global fellowship of social entrepreneurs. Al Etmanski was one of the first two Canadians selected to be part of this prestigious network.

www.cdss.ca The positive communications and strong ethical stances make the Canadian Down Syndrome Society a leading advocacy organization.

http://chance.unh.edu/ The Center for Housing and New Community Economics. Chance is dedicated to increasing access to integrated, affordable and accessible housing.

www.communityworks.info This is the website of David and Faye Wetherow, social inventors, trainers, and consultants.

www.fieldnotes.ca This is the website of Sandra Shields and David Campion. This talented couple have dedicated their writing, photographic and artistic talent to economic and social justice issues.

www.ilcanada.ca This is the umbrella organization for the Independent Living movement in Canada and a network of Independent Living Centres.

www.in-control.org.uk This website is testimony to the power of families and individuals with disabilities. In Control led the campaign for direct funding or self-directed support for the elderly and people with disabilities.

www.inclusion.com This is the website of Inclusion Press International and the great work of Jack Pearpoint, Lynda Kahn, Cathy Hollands, and the late, esteemed Marsha Forest.

www.laidlawfdn.org This website is dedicated to encouraging young people to become healthy, creative and fully engaged citizens. Nathan Gilbert and his team are major supporters of our Belonging Initiative.

www.larche.ca L'Arche is PLAN's closest collaborator, embodying and exemplifying the work of their founder Jean Vanier. It is worth subscribing to *A Human Future*, a quarterly electronic publication featuring thought provoking interviews with outstanding Canadians.

www.mcconnellfoundation.ca This website is the home of the progressive JW McConnell Family Foundation and long-time supporter of PLAN and the PLAN Institute.

www.normemma.com This website links to the talented, inspirational and humorous team of Norman Kunc and Emma Van der Klift who provide keynote addresses, workshops, and training in the areas of inclusive education and disability rights.

www.qualitymall.org This is a website where you can find free information about person-centered supports for people with developmental disabilities. Each of the "Mall Stores" has departments you can look through to learn about positive practices that help people with developmental disabilities live, work and participate in our communities and improve the quality of their supports.

www.sesp.northwestern.edu/abcd This is the home of John McKnight's Asset Based Community Development Institute.

www.tamarackcommunity.ca This website is full of resources and practical advice for community engagement, community organizing, and convening.

BC organizations

Autism Society of British Columbia

www.autismbc.ca

The ASBC is a parent based society providing support to individuals with autism and their families.

BC Association for Child Development and Intervention

www.bcacdi.org

The BC Association for Child Development and Intervention is a provincial association of agencies which provides child development and therapy services to children with special needs and their families in British Columbia.

BC Association for Community Living

www.bcacl.org

BCACL enhances the lives of children, youth and adults with developmental disabilities and their families by supporting abilities, promoting action and advancing rights, responsibilities and social justice.

BC Brain Injury Association

www.bcbraininjuryassociation.com

The British Columbia Brain Injury Association is a Provincial organization serving the interests of all British Columbians affected by Acquired Brain Injury.

BC Centre for Ability

www.centreforability.bc.ca

Its mission is to provide community based services that enhance the quality of life of children, youth, and adults with disabilities and their families, in ways that facilitate and build competencies and foster inclusion in all aspects of life.

BC Coalition for People with Disabilities

www.bccpd.bc.ca

The premier advocacy organization representing people throughout the disability community.

BC Paraplegic Association

www.bcpara.org

This association assists people with spinal cord injuries and other physical disabilities in achieving independence, self-reliance and full community participation.

CanAssist (Canadian Institute for Accessibility and Inclusion)

www.uvatt.org

This is the home of the Nigel Livingston and the University of Victoria's leading-edge technology program for people with disabilities and the engagement of thousands of students on disability matters.

Canadian Mental Health Association – BC Division

www.cmha.bc.ca

The Canadian Mental Health Association (CMHA), BC Division exists to promote the mental health of British Columbians and support the resilience and recovery of people experiencing mental illness.

Cerebral Palsy Association of BC

www.bccerebralpalsy.com

This organization works to raise awareness of Cerebral Palsy in the community; to assist those living with cerebral palsy in reaching their maximum potential; to see those living with cerebral palsy realize their place as equals within a diverse society.

Choice in Supports for Independent Living (CSIL)

www.health.gov.bc.ca/hcc/csil.html

Provides direct funding for purchase of in-home personal assistance. Contact Community Care Services or the Ministry of Health office in your community.

Coast Mental Health

www.coastmentalhealth.com

Coast operates the Coast Financial Trust program for mental health consumers who have Person with Disability status with the Ministry of Housing and Social Development.

Community Legal Assistance Society

www.clasbc.net

Provides free legal advice and representation on issues affecting people with disabilities.

Community Living BC (CLBC)

www.communitylivingbc.ca

This organization delivers support and services to people with developmental disabilities and to children with special needs and their families in British Columbia.

Down Syndrome Research Foundation

www.dsrf.org

This Foundation was formed in response to the need expressed by parents and professionals for detailed and research-based information for themselves and for the community at large.

Family Support Institute

www.familysupportbc.com

Canada's first family support organization for families who have sons and daughters with disabilities. Vickie Cammack was their founding Executive Director.

Infant Development Program of BC

www.idpofbc.ca

Serving children from birth to three years old who are at risk for, or who already have, a delay in development.

Ministry of Housing and Social Development

www.gov.bc.ca/hsd

This Ministry is responsible for BC Benefits, CLBC, employment, housing, and other programs impacting the lives of people with disabilities.

Nidus Personal Planning Resource Centre and Registry

www.nidus.ca

This website contains information about Representation Agreements.

The Public Guardian and Trustee of British Columbia

www.trustee.bc.ca

The Public Guardian and Trustee of British Columbia operates under provincial law to protect the legal rights and financial interests of children, to provide assistance to adults who need support for financial and personal decision making, and to administer the estates of deceased and missing persons where there is no one else able to do so.

Saferhome Standards Society

www.saferhomesociety.com

This is a resource for universal and safer design and building homes adaptable to the ever changing needs of people regardless of physical needs and age.

Self Advocate.Net

www.selfadvocate.net

Made by self advocates with disabilities built for self advocates with disabilities. This site has contacts with people all over Canada and the rest of the world. It is developed by and for self advocates with world wide links.

SET-BC (Special Education Technology)

www.setbc.org

Ministry of Education provincial resource program lending assistive technologies (reading, writing and communication tools) to ensure students' access to educational programs.

Society for Disability Arts and Culture

www.s4DAC.org

Based in Vancouver, the Society for Disability Arts and Culture (S4DAC) presents and produces works by artists with disabilities and promotes artistic excellence among artists with disabilities working in a variety of disciplines.

Society of Special Needs Adoptive Parents (SNAP)

www.snap.bc.ca

SNAP is a provincially registered not-for-profit and federally registered charity that helps families with challenges through mutual support, information, sharing, and advocacy.

Vela Microboard Association

www.microboard.org

This organization concentrates exclusively on developing micro boards for people with disabilities.

PLAN Books and Products

Visit www.plan.ca and click on "Resources" for a complete list of books and products from PLAN's e-store.

PLAN and PLAN Institute for Caring Citizenship offer products for sale. Please see below for a list of items and a brief description. To order, please visit www.plan.ca or www.planinstitute.ca.

The Company of Others

The Company of Others, a creative collaboration by author Sandra Shields and photographer David Campion, uniquely captures the spirit and significance of personal networks. Compelling stories and photographs lead the reader on an intimate journey into the lives of five individuals—with no connection to one other and little in common, except in one respect: each person is at the centre of an active social "circle"—a network of caring friends and family whose lives are enriched by the relationship they share. An extraordinary and moving book about the transformative power of family and community.

A Good Life

A Good Life for You and Your Relative With a Disability is an inspirational guide to rethinking disability and the value of people with disability in a caring society. It provides families, caregivers and those worried about the well-being of people with disabilities with insights, stories of inspiration, and practical advice. It offers a step by step guide to creating a plan for the future which provides for the safety, security, and well-being of people with disabilities.

Peace of Mind (CD)

The *Peace of Mind* CD-ROM is a practical and loving guide to help you plan for the future of your relative with a disability. It combines personal stories, testimonials, tips, and step-by-step worksheets to get you started on your path to peace of mind.

Reaching Out

Reaching Out by Nancy Rother, is a portrait of facilitated social network development across Canada. Filled with the wisdom of individuals, families, and facilitators from all walks of life, it is one of the clearest, most practical guides you will find on facilitating networks.

The Ties That Bind (DVD)

a National Film Board of Canada production

In *The Ties That Bind* award winning documentary, filmmaker John Ritchie takes a first hand look at a family's struggle to let go, when every instinct compels them to hang on. Richie follows the Jordon family—Kathleen, Bill, Chris and his two siblings—for almost three years. The result in an extraordinarily intimate film that reveals, with raw emotion and surprising humour, the complexity around one young man's transition toward a more independent life.

Peace Begins With Me

In *Peace Begins With Me*, Ted Kuntz shares the story of his journey of making peace with his son's disabilities. It is a journey through darkness to a life that is now filled with peace, joy, and happiness. At the core of Ted's message are simple yet powerful strategies that enable all of us to experience more peace and joy and create a life more of our choosing. A must read!